PREPARING

for the

KINGDOM

OF GOD

*True Divine Encounters
and Teachings from the
Lord Jesus Christ*

BOOK TWO

GLENN K VAN ROOYEN

Publisher: Preparing for the Kingdom Ministry; P.O. Box 340, Ennerdale, South Africa, 1826.

ISBN Number: 978-0-9968294-1-0

For information, contact:

Preparing for the Kingdom Ministry,

P.O. Box 340, Ennerdale, South Africa, 1826.

Online:

info@prepareforthekingdom.com I www.preparingforthekingdom.com

Cover photos: © ArvaCsaba / © Ig0rZh / Fotolia

First Edition: October 2016.

Acknowledgments

I would like to give a solemn and humble thank you to our Lord and Savior Jesus Christ for helping us produce our second book in less than one year. This second book carries the same title as our 'Book One' which we published in December 2015. Having said this, I am profoundly grateful to the Lord and blessed by this achievement.

I would also like to thank my wife Desiree for proofreading and helping me in every way to make this work possible. A special thanks to our daughters for their support, prayers, and patience.

I would further like to give due acknowledgement to some brethren in the ministry for persistently helping us with the cover design of this book and their countless hours of proofreading and editing. The laborious efforts of these brethren were priceless. Since we cannot repay them for their time sacrificed, we extended our thanksgiving to our Heavenly Father and trust that He will duly bless and reward them.

Finally, but no less importantly, we would also like to give a big thank you to our dear faithful friends and brothers in Christ, Messrs. Ryan Bird and Thom Hale for proofreading our manuscript and providing some useful advice and prayers.

Brother Glenn K van Rooyen.

Contents

CHAPTER 1

Leaning on God's Strength

"This is what the Lord says: Cursed is the one who trusts in man, who draws strength from mere flesh and whose heart turns away from the Lord. That person will be like a bush in the wastelands; they will not see prosperity when it comes. They will dwell in the parched places of the desert, in a salt land where no one lives. But blessed is the one who trusts in the Lord, whose confidence is in Him. They will be like a tree planted by the water that sends out its roots by the stream. It does not fear when heat comes; its leaves are always green. It has no worries in a year of drought and never fails to bear fruit" (Jeremiah 17:5-8 NIV).

Encouragement to Depend on God

In our first book, we introduced the Lord Jesus Christ as the Source of our message and the teachings we received from Him through revelation. Some of the teachings, which we shared in our first book, simply restated most of the teachings of the Bible. In Book One, we shared the importance of having faith in God and for our first discussion in this book, we would like to emphasize how pleasing it is to God when we show and express our dependence on Him. As Christians and followers of the Lord Jesus Christ, our dependence should be solely on God, and not on man or ourselves (Proverbs 3:5-6). For clarity, we will be sharing some real experiences from the Lord on this subject for your encouragement. It is worth mentioning right from the onset that the Lord Jesus Christ is ever aware of our every suffering and the challenges we each face as Christians (Hebrews 4:15). It is also true that some of our sufferings may stem from panic and fear, which forces us at times to be dependent on man instead of fully trusting in the Lord (Genesis 3:10). If we truly denounce or limit our dependence on the arm of flesh and choose to trust wholeheartedly in the Lord, and in His power and love for us, He will move the hearts of people to meet our needs. The Bible says that the Lord is true and faithful to His promise, and we are encouraged that He will never leave us nor forsake us (Hebrews 13:5). Therefore, our commitment to the Lord if well rooted in faith will enable us not to be moved or shaken by fear or panic. By this, we have a guarantee from the Lord to receive deliverance, provisions, and protection (Psalm 125:1). In his experience with God, King David assures us: *"I have been young, and now am old; yet I have not seen the righteous forsaken, nor his descendants begging bread"* (Psalm 37:25 NKJV). Additionally, it is common knowledge that the Christian journey or way of life is based on faith, and it would be safe to say that part of the "evidence" or proof of our faith has always been 'proven' by God's response in the natural to our needs through prayer (Matthew 6:4; 2 Corinthians 5:7; Mark 11:24). Without boring you with much detail, the gospels and the book of Acts are loaded with God's reply to the prayers of His faithful.

Godly Counsel in Needy Times

With the Holy Scriptures being our Source and guide to God's truth, the following Scriptural references show just how strong the faith of some people was and how they trusted in God for their protection and their needs:

- When King Nebuchadnezzar of Babylon gave an urgent order to execute the wise men of Babylon, Daniel did not panic in fear; instead, he and his companions trusted and sought God's favor to provide a way out of danger (Daniel 2:14-19).

- Similarly, when Sennacherib King of Assyria, threatened King Hezekiah, King Hezekiah did not go and make a treaty with some foreign army like King Asa had done before him (2 Chronicles 16:7-

9). Instead, he went to the Lord in prayer, God heard him, and the Lord rescued Him from the King of Assyria. (2 Kings 19:1-7).

- Additionally, the Lord answered the prayers of the Reubenites, the Gadites and the half-tribe of Manasseh and gave them great victory against the strong and powerful armies of the Hagrites, Jetur, Naphish and Nodab because they cried out to Him during battle and trusted Him (1 Chronicles 5:18-21).

- When King David was fleeing from Saul, he did not take matters into his hands to fight Saul; he sought Godly counsel in prayer, followed God's plan, and fled instead of inflicting harm on King Saul. If he had, that move could have greatly divided the Israelites (1 Samuel 23:12; Proverbs 15:22).

- Displaying a peaceful mood during arrest and persecution by the Roman soldiers, the Lord Jesus did not depend on His disciples' weapons for protection, but He trusted in the LORD God Almighty (Matthew 26:50-53).

Dependence on Men and Ourselves Yields Cursing

With so many learned speakers today, we often hear some popular statements such as "Believe in yourself" or "Trust in yourself." While these statements may sound quite encouraging and uplifting, as Christians we know in whose strength our faith must truly rest in (1 Corinthians 2:5). God has not called us to believe solely in our abilities, (2 Corinthians 10:17), but we are called to believe in the Lord Jesus Christ, for in Him we have given up our rights and surrendered to Him in full (John 6:29). Thus, we can do all things *through* Christ (not through others or ourselves) who strengthens us (Philippians 4:13). If it is only by our strength, then we glory in the flesh (Judges 7:2). The Bible admonishes us that *"It is better to trust in the Lord than to put confidence in man"* (Psalm 118:8 NKJV).

Using the Bible to clarify our message, there were some people who trusted in themselves or who followed ungodly ideas of men. In return, they received curses rather than blessings as the following Scriptures demonstrate:

- When King Rehoboam chose to take the bad advice of his young friends, Israel rebelled against him (2 Chronicles 10:10-19).
- When Nabal chose to return evil for good by not acting in kindness to King David's request, the Lord struck him down, and he died (1 Samuel 25:5-38).
- When King Ahab chose to listen to his wife's (Jezebel) wicked advice to kill Naboth and steal his vineyard, the Lord pronounced punishment and disaster for Ahab's family (1 Kings 21: 17-24; 22:37-38).
- When King David relied on his power and authority to get rid of Uriah the Hittite and took his wife Bathsheba, the Lord promised to raise evil against him from his household (2 Samuel 12:7-12).

God Cannot Be Ordered Around

I would like to start this heading with an experience I had. After my conversion in 1990, and being a new Christians, I fell into the habit of questioning the Lord regarding why He allowed certain things to happen to me. I wondered why He did not just prevent things from happening to me. In those moments of trial, I bitterly lamented that God was not answering my prayers! Back then, I panicked in fear of my situation just as the apostle Peter did (Matthew 14:30). However, as I persevered and matured in my faith, I realized that I could not just make demands on God to act as if I was ordering a servant. I learned to wait on the Lord patiently and with a humble attitude. We may safely add, that most Christians have some similar attitudes of simply giving orders to the Lord when they are facing steep challenges. One of the most popular, but false teachings advocated by prosperity teachers is that Christians have a right and entitlement to God's blessings. They are encouraged to "name it and claim it," demanding of the Lord to simply just give whatever material wealth or health we desire. As we emphasized in our articles on prayer in Book One, we must always, and in great humility and truthfulness, be patient and steadfast in our commitment, while we patiently endure the test until God intervenes and works in our favor. After endurance and being firm in our faith, the Lord will grant us deliverance (Daniel 3:18). In our experience and over the years, my family and I have learned to employ faith, patience, and humility to win God's favor. God responds to a humble request expressed in submission and faith (James 4:6). Additionally, the Bible teaches us that the fruit of patience slows our hasty temperaments, and it helps us focus on God's salvation and deliverance (Proverbs 14:29; 16:32). Some brethren who simply lack commitment regard consistent prayer as being laborious and wearisome. However, in our experience, we can confidently confess that consistent prayer brings forth trust, endurance, and it delivers patience to our faith (Luke 18:1-8). In various messages to us, the Lord expressed great satisfaction when we showed Him that we have faith in Him. In December 2013, when the Lord gave Charis (our daughter whom the Lord spoke to) a message for a faithful brother in our ministry, she recalled that she could sense the Lord's joy when He expressed His satisfaction with the brother's faith and, being pleased, the Lord granted some of his prayer requests.

In another experience earlier on in my Christian life, I briefly explained on our website how my retrenchment from a job I had in 1991 affected my faith and walk with the Lord. I endured some challenging and frustrating moments, which led me to take the easy way, that of relying on people's generosity to make ends meet. I later realized that I could not go back to people every time I had a need for basic supplies. However, some days after prayer and meditation on the Word, I decided to go on a three-day fast, and amazingly, after the fast, the Lord answered my prayers for a job.

In a similar experience, I was blessed by a testimony of a brother in the Lord who testified how he failed his motor vehicle driver's test twice because he depended on the 'mercy' of the officer to overlook his mistakes and give him a pass to obtain his driver's license. However, after realizing that he had made man his dependence, he repented and went on a one-day fast. Moreover, on his third attempt, the brother joyfully shared how the Lord fulfilled a promise He made to him a few months earlier in a dream that He would receive his driver's license.

Additionally, in several testimonies in our *Book 1* and on our website, I shared how depending on God for my family's needs has resulted in a great breakthrough for us. We are sharing a few encouraging verses from the Bible for your edification below:

- *"I lift up my eyes to the mountains — where does my help come from? My help comes from the Lord, the Maker of heaven and earth"* (Psalm 121:1-2 NIV).

- *"Trust in the Lord with all your heart, and lean not on your own understanding; In all your ways acknowledge Him, And He shall direct your paths"* (Proverbs 3:5-6 NKJV).

- *"Call on Me in a day of trouble; I will rescue you, and you will honor Me."* (Psalm 50:15 NIV)

Being encouraged by the above verses, we humbly implore you to put your trust and faith in God's hands. As a family who has experienced His love for people, we can convincingly testify that He will not overlook your situation as many think He does. God knows your anxious thoughts and CARES FOR YOU (Psalm 139:2; 23; 1 Peter 5:7). The Word says, *"Cast your cares on the Lord and He will sustain you; He will never let the righteous be shaken"* (Psalm 55:22 NIV).

As we conclude this chapter, we would like to re-emphasize and draw your attention to the kind of attitude God expects from His children, especially when asking of Him in our time of need. By asking of God, our attitudes should reflect a genuine trust and not on some pre-formulated prayers or dogmatism, nor should we look to some preacher(s) for answers. Instead, the Lord requires a humble attitude that is firmly rooted in faith from the heart.

I recall, a few years ago a brother shared with us how a young woman who, while lying on her sick bed, earnestly desired her pastor to pray for her healing. However, due to his busy schedule, the pastor could not make it on time to her bedside to pray for her. In her bitterness, she complained that her pastor did not care about her. Without being insensitive to her situation, this is exactly how some Christians react. They undermine their faith, and this precious sister did not value the worth and power of her prayers and that of other believers who were praying for her. She insisted for the pastor to pray for her healing. The point we are emphasizing here is that many Christians are not faithfully reading the Bible to learn that if we would only turn with desperation to the Lord, He who sees everything, is ever willing to intervene and remedy our demanding situation. However, a few weeks after her request for prayer to her pastor who never visited her, the young woman died without receiving her healing. We may conclude that her dependence and faith rested on her pastor's prayers and not on her faith and God's ability and promises to heal her. Sadly, this is the unfortunate situation of many Christians who put their dependence, hope and confidence in man and their dependency they are being piggybacked. Brethren, we should personally give our worries to the Lord, *"For we do not have a High Priest who cannot sympathize with our weaknesses, but was in all points tempted as we are, yet without sin"* (Hebrews 4:15 NKJV). We have witnessed and shared on our website in one of our deliverance articles how the Lord healed a very sick woman whom He only encouraged to pray for her healing and read her Bible. She obeyed, and the Lord healed her.

Frankly, we would like to emphasize that believers who are in the habit of relying on the faith of others will remain infants in Christ, and they will face many frustrating moments and disappointments. We encourage you to walk in the power of prayer and faith.

CHAPTER 2

Be Watchful and Pray

Be always on the watch, and pray that you may be able to escape all that is
about to happen, and that you may be able to stand before the Son of Man
(Luke 21:36 NIV).

Vision of Rapture, Warning Those Who Will Be Left Behind

In this chapter, we discuss our readiness for the Kingdom of God. We open with a vision from the Lord Jesus, which is a direct warning to the lukewarm and worldly Christians. The Lord Jesus Christ is coming soon! For your encouragement, the Lord Jesus Christ has personally warned my family to be always READY and WATCHFUL as no one will be receiving any 'special' warning on the timing of His coming. Being common knowledge, the Lord's coming in the form of the rapture will surprise everyone but those who are expecting Him, will not be caught by surprise (1 Thessalonians 5:2-4; Revelation 16:15). Let us therefore pray and be WATCHFUL!

Vision Given to Charis van Rooyen on June 28, 2015

"I had a vision from the Lord on the morning of June 28, 2015, after our morning prayers. I saw our ministry people and myself in our home church service with many other people I did not know. While I was looking through the entire congregation, and in an instant, I suddenly saw many of the people disappearing with only a few remaining behind; amongst those who remained were two members of our ministry team. I heard these two members yelling and screaming at the top of their voices saying 'the rapture took place, and we were left behind.' After realizing that they were not raptured, these two women started hurling abusive and hurtful insults at one another. I could sense that they were blaming each other for missing the rapture. While listening to them, the vision changed, and I saw further down the street many young children and other unsaved people in our neighborhood who also missed the rapture. From what I could perceive, these people were not even aware that the rapture had taken place, and they were just carrying on with their lives. When I looked at my body, it was all shiny, somewhat full of light. I knew that I was no longer part of this world and being left temporarily, I knew that I was there to comfort and encourage these two people and the others who were left behind (1 Corinthians 15:49; 51-52; 58). Without hesitation, I spoke up and said to them, *"Do not worry or lose hope because the Lord will be coming again* (referring to Second Rapture), *but your entry into Heaven will be much, much harder than the first time"* (referring to our present time). Although I spoke these words in the vision, the Lord put them in my mouth (Revelation 7:14). After my encouragement to them, a thought occurred to me in the vision that the devil will violently persecute Christians after the first rapture and that some will be brutally murdered and mutilated. When they face this torture, they must not deny the Lord and lose their salvation and entry into Heaven (Luke 17:33; Revelation 20:4). End of the vision."

As confirmation on two raptures, on October 13, 2014, I (Brother Glenn, you may read it on our website) received a vision from the Lord that there would be *two raptures*, one before the great tribulation and another during or after the great tribulation. In the vision above to Charis, the Lord confirms a second rapture and the severe hardship that disobedient Christians would face before entering Heaven if they overcome. Regardless of your beliefs on this subject (whether pre-tribulation, mid-tribulation or post-tribulation rapture), the point we are emphasizing is that you should be prepared for the Lord's soon coming.

Stay Alert and Pray

Therefore, as servants of the Lord, He commanded us to warn both Christians and unbelievers alike to be watchful and work out their salvation, and to live expectantly as if He is coming at any given moment (Revelation 22:12). Because the message concerning the Lord's coming has been preached since the time of the apostles, many people still disregard today's warning about the Lord's coming. We should *"Be alert and of sober mind. Your enemy the devil prowls around like a roaring lion looking for someone to devour. Resist him, standing firm in the faith, because you know that the family of believers throughout the world is undergoing the same kind of sufferings"* (1 Peter 5:8-9 NIV).

Given people's lack of faith and disregard for the word of God, we deem it necessary to remind you of the Bible's warning that we *"... must understand that in the last days scoffers will come, scoffing and following their own evil desires. They will say, "Where is this 'coming' He promised? Ever since our fathers died, everything goes on as it has since the beginning of creation.""* (2 Peter 3:3-4 NIV). In truth, the Lord has been confirming His soon coming to many other faithful and sincere brethren around the world, to comfort, warn, encourage and to cause us to focus on Him unswervingly.

Additionally, in numerous Scriptures, we are warned that the Lord's coming will occur suddenly and unexpectedly, like a thief in the night (1 Thessalonians 5:2; 2 Peter 3:10; Revelation 16:15). The Bible says people will be going about doing their business—eating, drinking, being entertained, marrying, and divorcing, etc., oblivious to the calamity that awaits, just like the days of Noah before the flood and the days of Sodom and Gomorrah and suddenly, the Son of Man will be revealed in great power (Matthew 24:37-41; Luke 17:28-35).

We are confident that the coming of the Lord is much closer and the rapture will take place in our lifetime. We base our confidence in our faith and watchfulness, and as further evidence, there are many confirmations from the Lord Himself through countless visions to many praying and faithful people, both saved and unsaved. On our website alone, we have shared warnings of the Lord's coming over a dozen times. Additionally, we have seen escalation in the fulfillment of prophetic events, for example (and this is only a very small fraction):

- Laws and judicial pronouncements are increasingly being passed legalizing sin (Romans 1:26-27; 2 Timothy 3:1-5; Isaiah 5:20).
- Several treaties and "peace" agreements have been made or are in the works (1 Thessalonians 5:3).
- The increase in false teachers and false prophets, many claiming strange gifts and focusing on materialism (2 Timothy 4:3-4; 1 John 4:1; 2 Peter 2:1).
- Increasing persecution of Christians who stand for Biblical truth (2 Timothy 3:12; John 15:19; Revelation 2:10; Mark 13:13).
- Signs in the sky (Joel 2:30-31) and on land (Hosea 4:1-3).
- Globalization and the massive increase of knowledge (Daniel 12:4).

Once again, brothers and sisters, we wish to reiterate that it is not our intention to stir up controversy or waste time arguing or creating quarrels about the Lord's coming and other Biblical subjects (2 Timothy 2:23; Titus 3:9). The essential point is this: the time to be ready is NOW because tomorrow is not promised. The day of one's death can come on any day (Proverbs 27:1; James 4:13-14). As we have experienced, the path to everlasting life is narrow and difficult (Matthew 7:14). People in the world may seem to have it easy on the wide road as they prepare themselves to embrace a new world order filled with false hope. However, as citizens of Heaven, we know that only the narrow road leads to eternal life (Matthew 7:13-14). Like the ten virgins, we may all grow weary and fall sleep, but please do not be like the five foolish ones who were not prepared! Our focus should be like the five wise virgins, having our lamps filled with oil and being Spirit-filled. This is achieved by maintaining a lifestyle of praying and the studying of God's Word. We should exercise a spirit of gratefulness, worshiping and of witnessing, and obedience to God. Therefore, when the Master suddenly comes, we will be ready and prepared to enter the promised Marriage Supper of the Lamb, don't you want to be part of it? (Matthew 25:1-13). We would like to share another rapture warning a vision that the Lord gave to my daughter.

Rapture Vision: Saved by One Minute

Given to Charis on July 9, 2014

"The Lord gave me a vision on July 9, 2014, after our early morning (6:30 AM) prayers. In the vision, I saw my mother, father and one of the sisters in our ministry team sitting outside in our car busy discussing something. My father and mother were sitting in the back passenger seats, while the sister in the vision was seated in the front passenger seat. On the driver's seat was seated a Black Figure (You may recall from our Book One who the black figure is) who rested his head on the steering wheel and his head was covered with a hoodie jacket. I got out of the house and walked to them. I opened the right-hand door panel of the car, and I sat next to my mother. Later, though, I laid my head on my mother's lap. It appeared to be very late at night, and it was very cold. As the conversation between my parents and one of our ministry sisters my aunt continued, I heard my father uttering a swearing word, and as he did, my right eye's focus was sharpened, and I saw a pair of black cards, which displayed a clock with time on it; it was *11:59*.

By the boldness of the Holy Spirit, I interrupted and shouted to everybody in the car, "Repent! Please Repent!" At that moment, I saw my father praying and he repented. In flash seconds, suddenly everything became silent everywhere in the world, and I heard the final seconds ticking by with the last second being very loud and the clock stopped and showed *12:00*. While I looked at the time, I noticed black clouds in the sky gathering, and I saw my entire family; all of us being caught up into the sky right into Heaven. When I looked down from above, I could see the sister who was sitting with my parents in the car still seated and left behind. Being disappointed, she threw her head back as she cried uncontrollably in a loud hysterical voice, *"I am left behind!"* *"I am left behind! I missed the rapture"* with the Black Figure still sitting next to her! Moments later in Heaven, I heard the Lord's voice saying to my father, *"You were saved by one minute!"* This was the end of the vision.

Many people think that they can sin and be worldly and once they see the signs of the Lord's coming they can repent. Be warned, you will miss the rapture and live to regret. The Lord said that His coming is near, but that many people are not ready! (Revelation 22:12, 20) People do not know when the last minute is, and many are taking the risk of missing the rapture by living sinfully. The Lord said that the sister in the above vision was left behind because she did not repent and her heart was still in the world and not on Him. The Black Figure (Satan) who sat next to the sister in the vision deceived and led her astray. The person who was saved by one minute is an illustration that only those who lived holy lives and repentantly at the time of the rapture will be saved. We need to remind you that our years of service in the Lord will not count in our favor when the Rapture takes place, but only those who are found faithful and ready will be saved (Matthew 24:13).

Brethren, we cannot overemphasize this fact that the Lord is warning Christians to be ready and live holy and repentant lives every minute of our service to Him, that we may be ready and worthy to see His face soon!

CHAPTER 3

Be Blameless and Spotless

"Therefore, beloved, looking forward to these things, be diligent to be found by Him in peace, without spot and blameless" … *"that He might present her to Himself a glorious church, not having spot or wrinkle or any such thing, but that she should be holy and without blemish."* (2 Peter 3:14; Ephesians 5:27 NKJV)

The Will to Resist Sinful Appetites

Christians face the inevitable task of confronting many struggles against sin and evil. Biblically, some of these struggles come through our own desires (James 1:15). To overcome these vices and cravings of sin, we need a strong will driven by faith and obedience. Our victory through the Lord serves as ring fence against sin (1 John 3:9). Therefore, the true mark of a born-again Christian is one's daily victory against the demands of sin (1 John 5:3-5). If we live a compromised Christian life by giving in to sinful advances and to please our worldly friends, we dishonor the Lord, and this affects the integrity of our salvation (1 John 3:7-10; Philippians 2:21). As a challenge to you, please answer these few questions honestly, to measure your sincerity and commitment to the Lord. Do you display bad fruit by being offensive and impolite without regard to how your actions affect other people? Do you often harbor wicked and hateful feelings against those who oppose you or correct you? Do you have a constant urge for worldly things and power to control others? Do you concern yourself more with things to please others rather than the Lord? Do you often lie to cover up your sins? Do you use excuses to avoid helping others? Are you often afraid to correct others when they have done wrong? Do you complain about almost anything? You may provide a simple yes or no answer, which would help you measure your attitude and conduct against the will of God. Now, in the light of these results, would you still rate yourself as being blameless? Let us consider the following Bible Scripture: *"Do everything without grumbling or arguing [complaining and disputing], so that you may become blameless and pure..."* (Philippians 2:14 NIV). This is a serious matter, for the Lord says that complaining people have an ungrateful spirit, and they do not show the fruit of peace. We may safely deduce that a well-balanced Christian life is measured against the teachings of God's Word. Wherefore, truthful living in Christ equals real freedom from guilt. And by being filled with the Word of God daily, we train and allow our self-will to submit to God's will, resulting in becoming a faithful and obedient Christian (1 Corinthians 13:4-8; Romans 12:9-21).

Judgment is Looming

Let us be reminded that Judgment Day is coming against those who practice evil and ignore the invitation to accept Christ (Romans 2:5-11; John 8:36). The Scriptures warns us that worldly riches, and being influential and having powerful friends with a high social status will count nothing on the day of reckoning (Proverbs 11:4; Zephaniah 1:18).

Without being ashamed, brethren, we purposely share this experience below to encourage you because our intention is to save people from the Lord's Judgements. As it is, we may learn something new from another vision the Lord gave Charis on September 29, 2014. On this specific evening, the Lord Jesus appeared to Charis and transported her in the spirit to a Heavenly Room. There, she was told in a vision the three most sinful habits that each person in our ministry (including some of our children who can distinguish between right and wrong) commits. After learning how our conduct displeased the Lord, we all humbled ourselves, wept, and prayed in heartfelt repentance. If we, as a ministry, who serve the Lord daily and with a devoted commitment are found lacking, how much more should those who are lukewarm and ungodly (1 Peter 4:18)? Brethren, let us remain set and focused on Christ, and be always repentant, being clothed with holiness so that we may escape God's judgments and be found worthy to enter heaven (Hebrews 3:15). Below, we are sharing a true vision of Hell for your edification and encouragement, and warning you against idolatry and worldliness (Colossians 3:5). Please beware and take heed.

Vision of Hell and Torments Inflicted on the Addicted

Vision Given to Jaydeen on April 27, 2013

"I heard the Voice of the Lord whispering into my ears: *"You are going to a place that is known to some people and unknown to others!"* At once, I saw Charis and myself laying on a bed, and our spirits left our bodies. We went to a very hot and dark place with screams coming from all around. This was my first experience of Hell, and I am reporting here as an eyewitness. I have no reason to lie or exaggerate on such an experience. On our trip to hell, we were accompanied by a tall and handsome looking Angel. As we entered Hell, the first thing we could feel was an intense heat. That place appeared to be completely dry with no moisture in the atmosphere. Our craving for water and fresh air was overwhelming. I could feel and hear sweat dripping from our faces and as it was about to evaporate it made a frying sound. Now, the very clothes on our bodies were on fire, without us being consumed.

The Angel, whose face appeared blurry, did not speak at all. He was only pointing us to the scenes and the people he wanted us to see and recognize. All the people we saw in the flames were in skeleton form. However, the faces of the people the Lord intended us to see and recognize were revealed to us. Some of the people we saw in the flames of hell were our very own close relatives. Some are long dead while others are still alive today, and the Lord sent us to those who are still alive to warn them that if they do not repent, the punishment we saw being meted out by demons below awaits them. Amongst the countless people and relatives that we saw, there were some whom I never knew or ever met. Upon inquiry, I learned that they had died long before my time. Furthermore, our attention was drawn to some activity taking place in front of us. We saw how demons were tormenting the people using the very habits they practiced while they were alive on earth (Galatians 6:7). When some of them were still alive in this world, we knew that their hobby of choice was excessive alcohol consumption and cigarette smoking. In hell, we saw different sizes and shapes of demons. These demons were throwing beer bottles at the people and pouring some liquid substance onto their heads, and this seemed to inflict terrible pain on them as it made them scream and with a sigh of some unbearable pain. I could also see how burning cigarettes were being pinned onto their heads by the demons, and their screaming seemed to amuse them because they were laughing. From what we perceived, this torment went on and on without end. As they were screaming and are tormented, we heard them calling the names of the people they knew. I heard them calling out for help saying: *"Glenn, Jaydeen, Charis help me, help me, help me please!"* Being in fear ourselves, we could only listen to their cry for help but could not do anything for them. After this scene and following the angel's instructions, we moved to another location, where we saw how a fat and very bald demon tormented a teenage boy, who appeared to be about seventeen years old. The young man was lying naked and face down in the flames of hell. We saw the demon who was assigned to torment him holding a long spear in his right hand. We saw the demon writing on the young man's back with the spear as if it was on pen and paper. The young man, who appeared to be in much pain looked at us while screaming, *'help, help, please help me!'* We saw words in one sentence appearing on his back, which were engraved in his blood, saying: *"Superga, showing off name brands"* (the Lord revealed the identity of the young man; we knew he had an unhealthy addiction to name-brand clothes and shoes). Immediately after this scene and our journey to Hell, words in bold writing appeared on our chests (Charis's, the Angel's and mine), wrapped in a white cloud: "A TRUE HELL STORY"."

CHAPTER 4

Persecution

Have you ever experienced backlash, slander, gossip, or backbiting on social media, or elsewhere because of sharing a godly message or warning? These are examples of persecution, which may be defined as opposition to God's will, and which includes harassing, falsely accusing, oppressing, hurting or even killing Christians because of their faith (Acts 8:1; Colossians 1:21). We would like to boldly state that Christians who persecute their fellow believers do not belong to the Lord, and His love is not made perfect in them (John 15:20; 1 John 4:8; 1 Corinthians 6:10). It is ungodly, utterly carnal and wicked for a Christian to attack his brother or sister in Christ verbally with the intent to hurt (I Peter 4:14). A brother shared with us how he had to endure a verbal attack from another Christian brother, whose ministry office completely contradicts his ungodly actions.

The Lord has commanded all Christians to be their brother's keepers, and that includes correcting our brothers and sisters in love when they do wrong (Matthew 18:15-17; Galatians 6:1; 2 Thessalonians 3:14-15). As one family in Christ, we are encouraged to love and pray for one another (John 15:9; Romans 12:9-21; Ephesians 6:18).

Truthful Conduct Results in Persecution

Let us consider the following verse from the Word of God, *"In fact, everyone who wants to live a godly life in Christ Jesus will be persecuted"* (2 Timothy 3:12 NIV). If we allow sin to rule us, we despise the truth and oppose or persecute those whose conduct is more righteous than ours (Genesis 4:1-7). Cain, like many of us, allowed sin to dominate him, and by considering himself inferior to his brother through a spirit of jealousy, his shame led him to murder his righteous brother, Abel (Genesis 4:8). When we consider the example, we observe that persecution comes from people who opposes righteous living (Jeremiah 28:8-17). Similarly, when the Lord Jesus rebuked the teachers of the law, they hated Him, and their natural response was to persecute and kill Him (Matthew 16:21). With so many churches and various false teachings around today, this has also awakened a spirit of persecution amongst Christians. Our present age has produced more divisions in the body of Christ and the persecutions amongst Christians seem to be a silent war, which has created doctrinal positioning in the church. In other words, each doctrinal grouping defends its own set of truths and convictions.

Why are Christians Persecuted?

Scripturally, it's been proven that everyone who speaks the truth in the name of the Lord and opposes wrong behavior, and deceitful teachings will face persecution (Matthew 5:10; 2 Timothy 3:12). As a ministry, we have endured persecution from both Christians and the unsaved alike, for being obedient to the Lord and exposing some lies behind certain popular teachings and practices in the Church. You may read all about these warnings and articles on our website.

Take comfort that *"all men will hate you because of Me, but he who stands firm to the end will be saved" (Matthew 10:22 NIV)*. Therefore, we may boldly declare that God's message appeals to those who love Him and choose not to live for themselves.

Persecution May Lead us to Stumble

Satan had succeeded in his first attempt to tempt man when he caused Adam and Eve to disobey God (Genesis 3). However, when he tried to tempt the Lord Jesus Christ with the intention of causing the Lord to disobey the Father we know that the Lord Jesus endured and overcame his advances (Matthew 4:1-11). Before the devil succeeds in tempting us, he would operate from knowledge of our cravings, and when we give in to the craving, we would have yielded to the temptation (Genesis 3:6). Our escape to overcome temptation lays in our ability to resist by exercising our choice to obey the Lord more than the craving (Deuteronomy 30:19; Joshua 24:15).

For better clarity, Satan knew that the Lord was fasting and that He was hungry (Matthew 4:1-3). Now since he knew the Lord's need, he capitalized on it and provided the temptation. Therefore, no temptation ever come about without a need or want for something. This fact is further revealed in the Bible where King David was tempted to commit adultery and murdered Uriah after sleeping with his wife when he had seen her bathing (2 Samuel 11:2b). Like our Lord, David could have resisted the temptation, but he chose to yield to the tempting situation, which resulted in an unpleasant consequence for him (2 Samuel 12). In like manner, Eve was tempted to eat the fruit from the forbidden tree because she *"saw that the fruit of the tree was good for food and pleasing to the eye, and also desirable for gaining wisdom, she took some and ate it..."* (Genesis 3:6 NIV). Being a master deceiver, Satan skillfully exploits our weaknesses and cravings for things and then issues temptation to highlight the benefit of acquiring the object as bait to make us stumble. Moreover, he also succeeds by subtly creating the evil desire so that we ignorantly think we have a need for something (Genesis 3:6; James 1:13-15). For instance, when we see someone having something we don't need or have, we desire to possess such a thing without us having any need of it. By yielding to temptation, we show obedience to the desires of the flesh, instead of obedience to God (Romans 8:7-8).

If we choose to obey God, the Word says, *"And God is faithful; He will not let you be tempted beyond what you can bear. But when you are tempted, He will also provide a way out so that you can stand up under it"* (1 Corinthians 10:13 NIV). On a point of correction, have you not heard or personally quoted the preceding verse when confronted by a challenging situation? What this Scripture reference assures us of is about God's faithfulness. We are being encouraged that God will give us strength to overcome when we are weak. In other words, He will not allow us to be led into temptations that we cannot overcome (Matthew 6:13). As we conceded earlier, temptations are bound to come (Luke 17:1), but not beyond the strength God has endowed us with. What we mean is this, God will not allow us to be tempted with the same measure of temptations as our Lord Jesus Christ was (Luke 12:48). Likewise, the apostles and prophets all had different strengths, callings, and ministries, based on their individual strengths which accordingly attracted its set of troubles and temptations (Luke 9:54-55). Truthfully, to overcome the undesirable occasion of temptation, we need to use our faith and discernment to recognize God's voice and not to yield (2 Samuel 24:10).

For the benefit of new Christians, please allow me to relate from my experiences. Before I accepted Jesus as Lord of my life, I used to smoke cigarettes and drank alcohol. Now, since I was familiar with the taste and pleasures of these habits, the craving to feed my addiction kept coming. However, after my conversion, I received the strength from the Lord to exercise my faith in obedience to Him (Romans 6:11-13; Genesis 4:7). Personally, by looking back to my days of addiction, not only did my habits affect my family but they also affected me physically, socially, and financially. There is no better way to present it than to say that people who are bound by these habits are often sickly and poor in many ways. This is evident in our society today.

Briefly, the wrong teachings in the church today which are advocated by the prosperity movement has presented Christianity as a "God does it all for me religion" maintaining that we only need to have faith and whatever we need will be given to us. True, if our motives and lives are right before God, He will hear our prayers and provide for our needs. Also, the Lord told us that the Father knows that there are people who only want to receive from Him, but they are not honoring Him with their lives. Some people think that faith is enough, never! The Bible says faith without works is dead (James 2:14-26). The prosperity teaching is being demanding; it only wants God to perform. We accept that the

Lord requires faith to provide for our needs, but using 'miracles' to attract people with the promise of expecting God's miracle when their lives are not right with the Lord is a total fraud. The danger is, if people did not receive what they expected from the Lord, they would go back to their former ways after they 'tried' God out. I would like to again use my experience again to illustrate this message. A few weeks after I accepted the Lord as Savior I was still in the habit of smoking and acting worldly. From the kind of sermons that I listened to by some prosperity teachers, I thought that I did not have to do anything on my part to kick my habits, but that it would simply just disappear after the pastor, or somebody else, prayed for me. By the teachings, which are still widely followed, I had been assured "just to have faith," and if I did not have faith, I would not receive my deliverance. From my own personal experience in the ministry, I have met and corrected countless people from this way of believing and thinking. Additionally, our experiences with the Lord Jesus has added to our understanding that people need to exercise their faith and add an effort to their convictions. This is achieved through obedience to the Lord and abstinence from wrongdoing. Many Christians still expect today that after prayer their problems would just melt away. Being a minister of the gospel, I counsel countless Christians who are struggling with sinful habits. This false presentation of the gospel is causing the Kingdom of God many, many souls. Christianity is not a "magic wand solution" that offers a quick-fix solution to problems. No! The Bible teaches that we grow up gradually and as we start bearing fruit God prunes us, and this occurs through test and sufferings (John 15:2). Naturally, we all expect answers right away, and we have this expectation that since we serve the Lord, we should not have any problems. On the contrary, there is no Biblical justification for that. The Bible says that we should patiently wait for the Lord as this world is filled with problems (Romans 8:25; John 16:33). In desperation, we have witnessed how this kind of expectation has led some people to repent with the false belief that God will take all their problems away. This is not the case; the Lord uses the problems we face to lead us to Him and to shift our dependence on Him (Jeremiah 33:3; Psalm 50:15). Realistically, this way of belief has led many astray and into false beliefs and religions.

As a ministry, we encourage all new Christians to read the Bible, pray daily, discern and listen to the Holy Spirit, bear the fruits of faith, be patient, endure, and exercise self-control (2 Peter 1:5-7). Salvation is a two-way effort; God requires our active participation in our salvation through our faith and submissive obedience to His will daily, and He grants us the grace to endure through the convicting power of the Holy Spirit (Colossians 2:6-7; Philippians 2:13). The Bible admonishes us to *"continue to work out [our] salvation with fear and trembling"* (Philippians 2:12 NIV).

Reasonable Service

Biblically, reasonable service to the Lord is offering our bodies as a living sacrifice in obedience (Romans 12:1). Let me pose you with a challenge, can we say we are completely free from all cravings? The answer is "No!" (Romans 7:15-25). But why? As long as we are present in this body, its passions will hound us (Galatians 5:16-21). We are free through Christ as far as our choice in submission to His Lordship and our obedience to Him are concerned. Strictly speaking, freedom from sin in this body will only come after this life (Romans 7). By this assurance, this does not mean that we should allow sin to dominate us. In fact, we have been given power over it (1 John 5:4; Luke 10:19). Satan's intention is to lead us sinning through temptations resulting in eternal death (Galatians 5: 16; Romans 6:23). In some other passages, the Bible says that when we are born again, we should lead a life of spontaneous and willful obedience to the Lord (Colossians 3; Ephesians 4:17-28). By this, we mean that we should consciously, and by faith, choose to "crucify the body" or put its cravings to death (Colossians 3:5-6). We should realize that indulgence in some forbidden activity does not only bring temporary pleasure, but it also invites a demonic spirit associated with that craving, consequences, and shame. About two years ago, the

Lord showed me in a vision how a spirit of lust entered and possessed someone who gave in to temptation, and he committed sexual sins. Not only did this act of disobedience hurt him, but his relationship with the Lord was affected. Brethren, we cannot emphasize this point enough: obedience and humble submission to God through faith equal deliverance and a future hope of eternal life (Psalm 31:23).

The Lord's Forgiveness and Compassion

Based on our experience with the Lord, we can assure you that He is aware of each one's struggles as it happens. We are thus comforted: *"He will also provide a way out so that you can endure it"* (1 Corinthians 10:13 NIV). This shows us that God foreknew and foresaw all troubles that may come our way, so He intervenes, *"For we do not have a high priest who is unable to sympathize with our weaknesses, but we have one who has been tempted in every way, just as we are- yet without sin. Let us then approach the throne of grace with confidence, so that we may receive mercy and find grace to help us in our time of need"* (Hebrews 4:15-16 NIV). Furthermore, the Word of God exhorts us that, *"You were taught with regard to your former way of life, to put off your old self, which is being corrupted by its deceitful desires; to be made new in the attitude of your minds; and to put on the new self, created to be like God in true righteousness and holiness"* (Ephesians 4:22-24 NIV).

Encouragement to Endure Persecutions

In concluding this chapter, we would like to encourage you to endure persecution prayerfully and faithfully. If you are currently facing persecution for standing up for God's truth, or you are afraid of being persecuted, fear not! Take courage and comfort in the promise and knowledge that the Lord loves you and His grace is sufficient for you (2 Corinthians 12:9). Absolutely nothing and no one *"...shall be able to separate us from the love of God which is in Christ Jesus our Lord"* (Romans 8:35-39 NKJV).

CHAPTER 5

Deception – The Power of Satan

We would like to consider the account of the Lord Jesus' temptation and that of Adam and Eve to better present this message about deception. When the Lord gave me this message through Charis to write, I did not know how to present it adequately, but after prayer, the Lord revealed to me how the devil's deceitfulness changed the world. Now, when Satan was tempting our Lord Jesus Christ, the Lord could discern the devil's duplicity and so He Scripturally resisted Satan's advances (Matthew 4:3-10). Subsequently, the Lord overcame Satan by proving to him that obedience to God's will is important. Conversely, the devil had succeeded in deceiving Adam and Eve, leading them to sin against the Lord (Genesis 3:4-5), which in turn had a lasting and enduring impact on nature and the entire human race (Genesis 3:17-19).

We can recall that the first message God gave humanity was to exercise a choice (Genesis 2:16-17). Satan, on the other hand, also provided a choice that went against the good counsel of God, resulting in a curse and hardship for all the earth (Genesis 3:4-19). Following the curse, the Lord God showed us that our choices would be limited and subject to His authority. The promise of Satan was *"You will not surely die"* (Genesis 3:4 NKJV), showing us that we have the power to resist God's will, and implying that there are no limitations and that we can just do as we please. In this encounter in Eden, the devil instinctively implied that God's authority does not count and that humanity should mark out their own destiny apart from God. This undoubtedly brought about the current conflict, which we all have within us: the conflict of good versus evil (Galatians 5:17).

Furthermore, the Bible explains that through the deception that Adam and Eve yielded to, sin possessed and permeated humanity (Genesis 6:5; Romans 5:12). As it is, this disobedience resulted in humanity becoming slaves to sin (Romans 6:18). Consequently, we became enemies of God about our conduct (Romans 5:10) by the force of sin fueled by *'the prince of the power of the air, the spirit who now works in the sons of disobedience'* (Ephesians 2:2 NKJV).

How Are People Deceived?

According to the dictionary, deception may be lying, tricking and purposeful dishonest behavior aimed at misleading others. To apply this duplicity to humanity, we may say that a deceptive person is not interested in truthful conduct and does not express any trustable values. Rather, such a person seeks opportunity in every situation to act contrary to truthful values. The Lord Jesus said that Satan, our enemy, acts naturally when he exhibits his talent—deception (John 8:44). To advance his legacy, he has defiled people everywhere in this world to replicate his dubious behavior (1 John 5:19). In explaining the spirit of deception in people, I would like to relate an experience. In late December of 2015, a concerned father asked me to pray and counsel his son, a young man of about 25 years old, who has a drinking problem. After our counseling session, I encouraged the young man in the Lord and, with his permission, I prayed for him. He promised to reform his ways but, a few days later, after recovering from his hangover, he went back to his former ways. A few days afterward, when I inquired from his father about his whereabouts, he started chronicling the behavior of the young man. From what I heard his father saying, the young man was in the habit of making false promises, smooth-talking himself out of trouble, lying, stealing, and using every kind of deceitful ways to achieve his goal of getting money to support his drinking habit. Now, this type of behavior is not isolated. In our ministry experiences, we have come across many people with a similar demeanor, and the Lord has pointed out to us as a warning that such people exhibit Satan's identity (John 8:44). What is evident is that such people act selfishly. Their goal is to gratify their fleshly desires and appetites.

Let us examine a little further, just how are we enticed to sin? Naturally, people always fall for things they see on the outside, and that is often the bait Satan uses to cause our fall (1 Samuel 16:7). This reminds me of an experience that I had with three of my childhood friends. About three decades ago, my friends and I were unemployed high school dropouts. One day as we were sitting and discussing ways to find employment, a man who seemed to be in his early thirties approached us. He was decently dressed in formal attire. As if knowing our need, he caught us by surprise and changed our moods to joy when he asked us if we were interested in working for him. Upon further inquiry and curiosity, he related to us that he owned a building construction company somewhere in Johannesburg, South Africa. Now, at that time we did not realize this, he must have overheard our conversation that we were looking for jobs. Since we had never been formally employed before, the salary he promised to give us could have tempted any broke and unemployed youth. He proceeded to ask if we had any money to use for our transport to the work destination, promising to refund us when his assistant arrived with the company truck. We gave him whatever cash we had on us, and we asked him to accompany us home so that we could go and fetch some clothes. After getting our belongings, we followed him on foot to a remote house about five kilometers (three miles) away. After he had introduced us to his girlfriend, he left saying that we should not go anywhere but wait for him, as he would return with the transport. To our disappointment, we ended up waiting for him the entire day. As night time approached, our hopes of ever seeing him again faded. Being concerned, we inquired more about him from his girlfriend and some of the people he had left us with, but they were tight-lipped and reluctant to give us any information. They did, however, provide us with food and a place to sleep for the night. Our strongest worry was no longer the money he took from us, but how we would face family and friends back home after having left in such a hurry with pomp and excitement. The next morning, when we realized that we had been duped and that we might never see him, we got up, took our bags and headed back home. I could still remember, as we were heading back home, I wished I could have just kept on walking forever without ever reaching home because of the shame and embarrassment. That day, we made peace with ourselves and accepted that the unknown man disappeared with our hopes and dreams of an employment opportunity to support us, and our needy parents.

Now, similarly, Satan is familiar with our shortcomings and things we desire, and he uses them to enter our lives. Once he gets in, he works to destroy us (John 10:10). In 1992, I met a friend who appeared impressive to me with his worldly knowledge and reasoning. This man was well versed in the Scriptures because of his Bible School training and his pastoral background. With his 'superior' and manipulative tactics, he made me doubt the Bible, saying he was reading books that challenged his intellect. During those years my main source of reading was the Bible, but his talk made me believe that the Bible was not a good source to stimulate thought. My desire for the Lord slowly died, and I desired the 'knowledge' he had where he simply had an answer to almost anything. By opening my soul and allowing this new knowledge to infiltrate me, it shook the foundations of my faith, and doubt started building up in me, which made me question the authenticity of the Bible. Sooner, I abandoned my usually habitual Bible reading and praying. My fall was hard as I descended into faithlessness and discouragement. What was evident to others who knew me is that they noticed that my joy and encouraging spirit was gone. All I had left was confusion and an endless disturbance on the inside.

The Lord, being familiar with my dilemma, surprised me one night around February 1992: I had my first ever vision of the Lord Jesus. In the vision, He appeared in shiny white clothes and sat on the bedroom dresser seat. In the vision, I was seated on my bed and in a thought transference conversation, He said: *"Be careful not to believe anything that anybody tells you; just believe the Bible."* I knew the Lord was addressing my doubtful concerns and confusions. I had also battled with the question regarding the authorship of the book of Hebrews, after reading conflicting reports on this Bible book. Through the thought transference conversation, I asked the Lord only one question: "Who wrote the Book of Hebrews?" Without hesitation, He answered saying that the apostle Paul was the author. Just as the Lord got up to leave, I spontaneously seized His right hand and brought it closer to my eyes; it was then that I saw a wound inflicted by the nail of His crucifixion. Being familiar with my moment of weaknesses and the perfect timing of His visitation to me, He could not have come at the right time, especially when my faith was shaken. Indeed, His visit to me was perfectly timed when the seeds of deception were having a negative outward effect on my relationship with Him. By then, my prayer life was nonexistent, and my Bible reading had taken a huge nosedive. As a 'Christian' then, I operated simply on belief and knowledge, with no fruit to add to my faith, which is the worldly way of faith—go to church, carry the Christian title, and live in sin (Matthew 3:8; 7:19).

Admittedly, this visitation by the Lord did not have an immediate impact on me, but the Lord's words that I should trust in the Bible remained with me. Because this was such a good experience, I recorded this in my personal journal. As my relationship with the brother who deceived me continued, so did my downslide path. Through his persuasive speech, the same brother led me to believe that having a little wine was not a sin, even pointing to some Scriptures. Consequently, I ended up drinking until the habit was completely formed in me. With that, gone was my innocence; I simply 'graduated' to being a full-blown social drinker with no time to for God, let alone Bible reading. To ease my conscience, I only attended Sunday church services. Brethren, this experience that almost cost me my salvation and soul, serves as a serious warning! There are folks out there who have great Bible knowledge, and some of them use the power of their knowledge to deceive and control the unsuspecting novices in the faith. Those are agents of Satan working against the will of the Lord, just as the devil tried to use his knowledge of the Bible to deceive the Lord (Matthew 4:6). There is NO substitute for Bible reading, and we cannot emphasize this point enough: Please keep reading your Bibles! This is how we wise up in our knowledge of Christ and overcome the temptation of being deceived (Proverbs 4:20-22) *"that we should no longer be children, tossed to and fro and carried about with every wind of doctrine, by the trickery of men, in the cunning craftiness of deceitful plotting"* (Ephesians 4:14 NKJV). If I had known the Scriptures then and followed its convictions, I would have been empowered to resist these sinful advances and temptations. Evidently, my downfall was largely due to my lack of faith and ignorance of the Bible (Hosea 4:6). Today, many believers are deceived because they do not read the Word of God for themselves and, sadly, some live their Christian lives by every preaching and teaching of their pastors without verifying the truthfulness of the message in the Bible (Acts 17:11). We are by no means asserting that it is wrong to listen to the preaching of the Word, but we strongly encourage you to read and study the Scriptures for yourself while testing what's being preached (1 Thessalonians 5:21).

Bible Knowledge Conquers the Deceitfulness of Ignorance

To understand the web of deceit and Satan's master plan to destroy Christianity, let us consider the fact that he has managed to create many sects within Christendom to advance the spirit of confusion and divisions amongst Christians. His primary targets are those who are ignorant of the Scriptures, those disadvantaged by illiteracy, and those who do not have time to read their Bibles. By the Lord's personal messages to many members of our ministry team and many others, their obedience to Bible reading and Scriptural living while praying persistently daily has yielded them personal blessings, peace and a greater understanding of the ways of truth. It is a spiritual tragedy if we would choose to dance to the "superior" Scriptural knowledge and influence of those we call leaders. What we mean by this is if we willingly just accept a teaching without verifying it against the Bible and our discernment based on our knowledge of the word, we might end up being deceived. In the Lord, all Christians have been discouraged from displaying any form of superiority (Matthew 20:26; 23:11). In our concern for your salvation, dear brethren, we humbly encourage and challenge you to study the Scriptures for yourself daily starting from Genesis to Revelation. Please, obey its commands and instructions, and pray, asking the Lord for wisdom to properly understand the Scriptures (James 1:5). As many Christians have discovered, the result of such devotion should open your eyes to see the many errors and deceptions afflicting the Church today. You may be assured that you will be firmly rooted, solid as a rock in Christ, unshaken in your faith (Matthew 7:24-27; Ephesians 4:13-14; Psalm 62:6). For further discussion on the importance of Bible reading, you may refer to our recent article on our website titled *"Maturing as a Christian."*

Persecution is from Satan

To expose the source of persecutions, the Lord gave us a vision regarding Satan's schemes. On March 22, 2013, Jaydeen, one of our daughters, was shown a vision of a young woman who desired to serve the Lord along with her two boys. The Lord was showing how her husband, through the working of Satan, opposed her faith in the Lord. In the vision, Jaydeen saw this young mother listening and singing to worship music that was playing in the background. In her devotion, there were three pages of handwritten prayers lying on the table, which she had written. Her husband, who is a Muslim, suddenly entered the house while she was still busy worshipping. When he saw what she was doing, worshipping the Lord, his face changed to an evil appearance, and in a rage, he charged forward, grabbed the prayers off the table, browsed through them, and he then started tearing up these prayers. As he tore them up while shouting and yelling at his wife, who appeared to be in great fear of him, he demanded, *"What is this nonsense?"* At once, I saw the Lord come down from Heaven in dazzling white clothes with His face covered in a cloud, and standing next to me (Jaydeen), He spoke and said, *"The devil is inside this man, and the devil is standing next to this man."* The Lord revealed to us that those who persecute the truth and the gospel have the devil inside of them, and Satan is commanding them to do his will (John 13:27). It must be noted, that this was the same anger and hatred Satan stirred up against Stephen and the Apostle Paul because they spoke in the name of the Lord (Acts 7; 21). While Satan and his servants use brutal force and violence to subdue people, the Lord uses His merciful love to attract all humanity (Matthew 11:28).

The Lord's Second Coming

Let us turn to the Christian hope, the Lord's Second Coming is another hotbed of deception. If you are a seasonal Christian, you are in danger of missing the rapture! I say this because the Lord has revealed to us that many Christians are deceived in thinking that they will make their lives right with the Lord when certain 'signs' take place. They are information seekers who 'repent' when they have noticed a 'sign' of the Lord's coming. When they discovered that it was a false alarm, they return to their former ways and relax their devotion. Now that is a very serious game they are playing, for sudden destruction might just strike (1 Thessalonians 5:3). That is why the Lord has warned Christians not to predict falsely and point to signs that only He knows or allows to happen. The coming of the Lord Jesus Christ is near and He has told us that He is coming soon. We are in the end-times, but beware: The Lord says no one knows the day, nor has He given anyone the wisdom to unravel the times and accurately point to a specific sign like He did through the wise men and the teachers of the law (Matthew 2:1-12; 1 Thessalonians 5:2; 2 Peter 3:10). So, do not be deceived by those who offer certain signs; just stay focused and be ready always. I encourage you with words that the Lord Jesus gave us: *"Don't worry; just believe and be faithful. I am coming soon!"* What we have shared here is a warning to those who follow signs and hope to repent when they see these signs; the Lord has warned that they will be caught off guard! (Matthew 24:36-44). We share another eye-opening vision; be ready to discern and learn.

Vision of Satan and His Influence on People

Vision Given to Charis on April 5, 2013

"I had a vision from the Lord after our early morning prayers. I was in a very dark room with a dark figured man who had his face blurred out. He had a blue tie, white shirt and grayish pants on. The room was pitch dark, but there was a ray of light coming from the Lord that was just shining on him. He spoke up and said to me: *"Do you know how much the Devil really hates you?"* I replied and said, "Yes, I do know." He continued and said, *"But you never experienced it. Come, let me show you four things on which the Devil works through people. I am going to show you your family."* The man then turned on what looked like a flat screen TV.

First, I saw Freddy (not his real name), a 13-year-old boy who is a close relative, appearing on the TV screen and my father (Glenn) was standing to his left. I saw the devil standing to Freddy's right-hand side, and I heard him whisper into Freddy's right ear *"LIE! Lie! Lie!"* I noticed those words echo into his left ear, *"LISTEN, listen, listen!"* Immediately he obeyed the voice of the devil and started to lie to my father.

Next up was Jaydeen. My father was busy rebuking her for wrongdoing, and the devil was standing next to her, and also whispered into her right ear, *"Have an attitude, be rude and think that these people hate you and are treating you bad."* and her other ear also started echoing *"Listen, listen, listen!"* As if being programmed, she immediately started acting just as the devil commanded her. I noticed how her appearance changed from being jovial to being sad with an angry look. The devil appeared to be very impressed with her change of attitude.

Next up was my mother. I saw my mother appearing on the screen, and she was about to serve us supper. My mother was about to open the microwave and the devil to her right was saying, *"Give Charis little food and a small portion of meat with an angry attitude."* I noticed the devil's voice whispering and echoing through her left ear, *"Listen, listen, listen!"* My mother responded in like manner; I received a small portion of meat, and when I politely asked for more, she became angry.

Then came my turn (Charis). Feeling upset by my mother's attitude, I went to my room and closed the door. The devil stood next to me and said, *"Feel sorry for yourself and have an attitude."* And this was exactly how I responded. I felt sorry for myself, and I was crying and had an attitude. The dark figured man spoke and said, *"I know I said only four things, but I want to show you one more thing how the devil influences even young children."* After he had spoken, I saw my then six-year-old sister, Claudia appearing on the television screen and the devil to her right. She was standing in our living room next to a plant in a jar and the devil said, *"Be rude and disrespectful to Charis and influence your mother to take your part."* Immediately, I saw Claudia leaving the house going outside and, as she left, she started hurling insults at me and answering me rudely and disrespectfully. I responded by rebuking her and reported her to my mother. Claudia lied and denied everything, leading my mother to believe what she said, and mom ended up siding with her.

The man then switched off the TV and shouted in a loud voice: *"COME HERE!"* I obeyed, and as I stepped forward, he violently pulled me forward by my clothes and threw me around the room as I felt powerless. By the force of his strength, I appeared to be weightless. As he was beating me, the Lord prevented me from feeling any pain. Unexpectedly, an open Bible appeared on my chest. It flipped and opened to Romans 12 and the devil tried to take it out, but he could not. He angrily beat and pulled me while screaming, *"I hate you! I make images in people's minds; I hate you! And I am the DEVIL!"* By faith, I said, *"Devil, I rebuke you in the name of JESUS!"* Instantly, he disappeared and left his clothes behind. After he had disappeared, I looked around the dark room, and I saw a mirror. I noticed how bruised and badly beaten I was; of the visible wounds, I had a black eye and scars all over my body."

In this vision, the Lord is revealing to us that Satan is the source of confusions, quarrels, lies, hateful feelings and deception (John 8:44; 10:10). Next time you see yourself or other people behaving wickedly, recognize that the devil is behind it all and rebuke him in Jesus' name while being polite to those who were influenced by him.

CHAPTER 6

Why Fasting is Important

"Now, therefore," says the Lord, "Turn to Me with all your heart, with fasting, with weeping, and with mourning." (Joel 2:12 NKJV)

Throughout the world, there are countless Christians who are needy, afflicted, suffering, and yet disobedient. The Lord has instituted fasting as a way of helping us to express our deepest need and faith in Him (Isaiah 58:1-12). If we have an earnest desire for His will and attention, the Lord will faithfully hear us (Psalm 10:17; 34:17; 18:6; 116:1; Jeremiah 33:3). Fasting is an essential Christian way of living, and true fasting should never be done to please man, but God. Also, we should not pursue fasting merely as a religious duty without a godly motive. When we fast, some of the reasons might be:

- To express remorse for our sins and for repentance (Jonah 3:6-10; Nehemiah 1:4-11).
- To seek help and express our dependence on God (Esther 4:3, 16; Nehemiah 1:4-11).
- To plead with the Lord to delay or reverse a pending judgment and grant His mercy (2 Samuel 12:16-18).
- To seek deliverance from demons and strongholds in our lives (Isaiah 58:6-7; Matthew 17:21).

In the Old Testament, fasting was mostly done corporately, while others fasted individually for mercy and repentance. In the New Testament, fasting is mainly done as a personal commitment (Mark 2:20; Acts 14:23); this will be the focus of this chapter.

Fasting That Pleases God

For Christians, fasting should always be preceded by repentance. During fasting, we confess our shortcomings and reliance on the Lord (Daniel 9:4-19). In his fasting, the Prophet Daniel was not self-seeking. Instead, he was seeking the will and the blessing of the Lord for his fellow Israelite brethren. Consequently, his fasting was accepted, his prayers were heard, and God answered him (Daniel 9:20-27).

Our Lord Jesus Christ prayed and fasted 40 days and nights for the work He was sent to do (Matthew 4:2), *"...and was heard because of His godly fear..."* (Hebrews 5:7 NKJV). As it is, when fasting, we should not place a demand on God to meet our requests. Instead, His will, purpose, and glory must be evident (Proverbs 25:2; Judges 20:26-36). In other words, our fasting must not be merely for selfish gain but for things that are important to God (Isaiah 58:1-12). When our Lord Jesus Christ fasted and prayed for those 40 days with loud cries and tears, He was armed with God's will and ready to serve to please the Father (John 6:38; Hebrews 5:7; 10:7). His commitment in fasting was not casual, but He fasted to preach the gospel, set the captives free, heal the sick, and open the eyes of the spiritually blind (Luke 4:18-19). The Lord's fasting was out of obedience and submission to the Father (Hebrews 5:8-10).

In reading the Bible, it is evident that fasting and prayer are inseparable. I know of many people who said they were on a fast, but without praying. That is neither effective fasting nor purpose-driven; our fasting must be for something specific (Esther 4:16; Daniel 9:2-3). I have also observed some people following a call for fasting and simply joining in without seriously committing their hearts in prayer for a specific cause. Fasting is a personal matter (Matthew 6:16) that should never be forced onto believers. When doing group fasting, as in Esther's case, we fast about things that affect all of us, and as individuals, we fast for things that we need, including the needs of our families and communities. I would like to emphasize that fasting alone cannot cleanse us from sin. Biblically, we may fast for deliverance from demonic oppressions and strongholds (habitual sins that control and corrupt our behavior) (Matthew 17:21). We are cleansed from sin and purified, through confession, by the blood of our Lord Jesus Christ (Hebrews 1:3; 1 John 1:7-9; Romans 10:9-10). This is our purification, the blood through the CROSS! Praise the Name of our Lord Jesus Christ! Below are brief testimonies on fasting and how the Lord blessed and delivered many people. When the Lord gave us these visions and testimonies, He did so purposely so that we may share with you for your edification and spiritual growth.

Fasting as a Test of Obedience

On July 12, 2013, the Lord commanded Charis that she and three members of her fellowship group fast for one day and do four prayers during their fasting. Now, the Lord did not say what they should specifically fast about, so they worked out prayer requests to place before the Lord. After their fasting the following day, the Lord congratulated them for being faithful in fasting, and He promised that He was going to bless them and that this fasting was a test of their obedience to Him. Without being aware, the devil tempted them to eat. In the vision, the Lord showed Charis how the devil strategically placed food to cause them to eat and disobey, but their obedience proved stronger, and this was very pleasing to the Lord. He had the four of them stand next to each other, and He said, *"I am really going to bless you all for being obedient."* As the Lord uttered these words, she saw how these words turned into a sound wave and entered both their ears. The vision changed, and the Lord made them feel a hot sensation on their cheeks as an indication that they each had received a kiss from the Lord for being obedient. I can, therefore, witness that the Lord did bless all of them generously on their birthdays with some money which He instructed us to give *'from My money'* (the ministry funds), as well other blessings.

As we shared previously (in Book 1 and in an article on our website titled *"Prayer is the Key to Solving All Problems – Part I and Part II"*, the

Lord instructed us (my wife, Charis, and I) to fast for just one day when we were on the verge of having our house repossessed by the bank. After the one day of fasting, the Lord again commanded us to pray for a full month. Like the prophet Daniel, the Lord heard our prayers, and we did not lose the house. At the end of the one month of prayer, the Lord concluded the matter and said that the house was now in His hands, and He commanded us to "DO NOTHING" more. We obeyed, and today we have a testimony to share with you from the same house. HALLELUYAH! As it turned out, the Lord blessed me with a job. The bank also called us, having withdrawn a court notice to foreclose, and negotiated a new and better deal with us without any input from us. We knew that the bank was acting on the Lord's instructions.

Additionally, a few years ago when I was in bondage to smoking, I fasted a full seven days for deliverance from this habit, and I received my deliverance that same week. Since smoking is a self-inflicted habit, I needed faith and obedience to work together with the Lord to deliver me, and He did. Those who are cigarette smokers or former smokers know what a troubling, traumatizing and tormenting habit this can be. I bless the Lord for the victory! In a message to a faithful brother and family friend who desperately needed a breakthrough, the Lord said, *"My son R must fast and pray if he needs something. And I love My Son R"*.

Fasting to Receive Gifts for Ministry Service

Without being aware that the Lord was calling us into the ministry, He commanded us back in February 2010 saying, *"You and your mother and father must go on a fast and I will tell you tonight about the fast."* When the Lord visited us that night, He said that He was going to bless us with gifts for ministry work, but we needed to fast for one day so that He could reveal the kind of gifts He had for us. Now brethren, it was necessary for us to fast and know the gifts from God so that we could add our faith to the gifts. No gift from God operates without faith (Romans 12:6); the fasting command from the Lord was to draw our faith to the gift. However, I will not draw attention to what gifts we received here, except to say that we are and have been using some of those gifts to serve in this ministry. We will also add that when the Lord was about to deliver the gift for Charis, He said, *"I am going to give you the best gift you ever had."* She received the gift of hearing mighty words and visions from the Lord, along with wisdom.

When this ministry started, the Lord commanded me to find five people to pray with, and as a reward for their obedience, He directed us to go on a three-day fast. After the fast, He granted each person's request. Those who were unemployed obtained jobs, others received the gift of speaking in tongues, and some received healing and deliverance.

The Lord is not pleased when we disobey Him or ask for something when we are not serious about it. Three young men once came to our home church asking us to pray for them for jobs and deliverance, and we took their requests to the Lord in prayer. He commanded that they pray and fast for one day. After their fasting, we received feedback that one of the young men did not obey and fast, so he did not receive anything. The other gentleman fasted, but he did not have faith in the Lord, so he could also not receive anything from the Lord. However, one brother received a full package of God's blessing due to his faith and obedience, and the Lord was very pleased with him. This same brother is still serving the Lord faithfully today.

Vision of an Answer to Fasting

On July 15, 2013, the Lord commanded Charis and the three other children in her age range to fast for one day. They obeyed, and the Lord answered in a vision and blessed some of them for their obedience.

Vision Given to Charis on July 26, 2013

"I had a vision, on July 26, 2013, after our morning prayers, of a woman, whom I know as Celeste (an Angel), who was sent by the Lord. We were in a white room, and I saw the angel was wearing a white dress and she had natural, brown hair. This was the second time the Lord had sent her to me. She said, *"Hi! Do you remember me"*? I answered and said,

"Yes, I do!" I saw myself and the three other children in this white room, and she turned to the one girl to my right and said, *"You prayed and did not want to go to a certain school next year (2014). Your request has been granted; that was your blessing."* (We can confirm that her application for acceptance for 2014 was unsuccessful, and the Lord granted her request, as this was against her and her mother's will.)

She then turned to the other girl and said, *"Your blessing is that you act obediently and receive less spanking; you also received a blessing for your birthday"* (this girl was personally blessed by the Lord with money, which was used for a party and a gift she needed).

After that, she turned to the boy and said, *"Your blessing has been coming on slowly because you are not working faithfully on your salvation."* The boy insisted that the angel tells him what blessing he got, and she said, *"You failed the previous quarter, but your blessing was you passed the last quarter"* (this young boy had been afflicted with every kind of disobedience in not doing school work, including neglecting to read his Bible and praying faithfully).

It was my turn (Charis), so she said, *"Your blessing is still coming, and it is going to be a very big blessing"* (While the Lord did not reveal in this vision exactly what Charis's blessing was going to be, she was very blessed on her birthday with a soul-moving message from the Lord. He also commanded my wife and me to give her a generous financial gift from our ministry funds). After the Angel Celeste had delivered the Lord's message to us, she waved us goodbye, and the door closed behind her."

CHAPTER 7

Courage is Expressing Faith

"Have I not commanded you? Be strong and courageous. Do not be afraid; do not be discouraged, for the Lord your God will be with you wherever you go"
(Joshua 1:9 NIV).

Courage is One of the Greatest Casualties of Faith

In the Bible, we can recall a few examples of people who experienced failure in their courage and how this led them to disaster. For example, Moses sent out twelve spies to explore the Promised Land of Canaan. Upon their return, the spies displayed some of the rich produce from that land. They also reported how powerful the inhabitants of Canaan were. They saw giant-like people there, descendants of Anak. Except for Joshua and Caleb, the spies presented the report in such a negative and unfaithful manner that the people got discouraged, and their hearts failed, so that they longed back to the days of bondage (Numbers 13: 1-33; 14:1-4).

Even though Moses, Caleb, Joshua, and Aaron pleaded with the community to trust in the Lord and not to be afraid, the people were determined to turn back in disobedience (Numbers 14:5-10). Not forgetting that this same rebellious community had experienced the mighty acts of God's judgments upon the Egyptians, and yet they still doubted Him. Consequently, they were driven by fear and gave up. The Lord forgave them and promised judgment for their lack of faith, and we know that He fulfilled the judgment He promised them (Joshua 5:6). I encourage you in the Mighty Name of our Lord Jesus Christ never to turn back to your old life of bondage after having experienced the Lord's deliverance. The devil is waiting for your return to the world to destroy you (Numbers 14:21-30; Matthew 12:43-45; Luke 9:62; 2 Peter 2:20).

God is Our Source of Courage

God the Father says, *"Fear not, for I am with you; Be not dismayed, for I am your God. I will strengthen you, Yes, I will help you, I will uphold you with My righteous right hand"* (Isaiah 41:10 NKJV). Furthermore, Joshua, being a man of faith, took God's Word literally, when the Lord said to him, *"Be strong and courageous, because you will lead these people to inherit the land I swore to their forefathers to give them. Be strong and courageous. Be careful to obey all the law My servant Moses gave you; do not turn from it to the right or to the left, that you may be successful wherever you go"* (Joshua 1:6-7 NIV).

As it turned out, Joshua took faith in the words of the Lord and God's command to be strong and courageous, and he brought the Israelites into the Promised Land (Joshua 24:8-14). This was a combination of faith, courageous leadership, and obedience, which resulted in the fulfillment of the promise. Therefore, faith is expressed through courage when facing uncertainty. I am not talking about human courage that seeks to elevate human strength and abilities. I am talking about taking courage in God's abilities, who drove out the mighty armies before the children of Israel. If we express such faith, God would be recognized as the Source of our achievement, rather than us. The result is always supernatural victory and beyond human ability (Joshua 1:3-9).

Courage is also often mistaken for risk nowadays. The world encourages people to take risks by experimenting their strengths and weaknesses. Therefore, the fruit of their effort is rewarded through wealth and self-glory. From a secular perspective, when non-Christians take risks they base their faith in their own abilities and not in the Lord. In our relationship with Lord, however, we express our courage by faith in God's abilities for His glory and our deliverance. In other words, we say, "Lord you say, so we do" (John 15:14).

On many occasions, we have witnessed how fear usurps a Christian's courage. In the example of Joshua, he had faith, but he needed to have courage as well. In the Bible, we also learn how fear seized upon people who lost their courage and ultimately gave up (Numbers 14:4). Although most of the Israelites of Joshua's generation fell in the desert, God used Joshua's courage to bring their children into the Promised Land. Likewise, God wants us to take up the courage of Joshua, Paul, and Peter as a testimony to trust in His ability. We read how they overcame all adversities as they courageously witnessed without fearing man (Acts 4:33). They had the courage to face prison, ridicule, and death, and yet they persevered (2 Corinthians 11:23-33).

Comparatively, today many Christians are discouraged to witness because they fear what others might think about them. They fear being rejected and ridiculed more than having the heart to witness and to save souls. In our experience, we have often witnessed how some lukewarm, disobedient, and self-righteous believers hurl insults to truly obedient believers by branding them as, 'fundamentalists,' 'Jesus freaks,' etc. God has promised to deal with mockers (Proverbs 19:29), and we must not lose our courage because of insults, offensive opinions, and abuse, for our work, is from God and by the conviction of the Holy Spirit (Acts 5:29). Let us, therefore, keep marching on in obedience and inherit God's promises (Joshua 1:7; Luke 6:22-23). The Lord has promised great rewards to the courageous and obedient believers (Revelations 3:21). Additionally, do not let your courage fail because you see many Christians befriending the world and living contrary to the Scriptures. Don't join in, but hold on faithfully to your confidence (Hebrews 10:23; 1 Corinthians 15:58).

We should all desire the God-pleasing courage of King Josiah who, when he heard about God's judgments, repented, and led his entire kingdom to national repentance (2 Chronicles 34:33). In his zeal for God, King Josiah took God's word literally and acted in obedience to it. He was led by a strong conviction and committed himself to follow the Lord with all his heart and soul. More so, he was possessed by fear for God and he followed the commands of the Word (2 Chronicles 34:31). He showed contempt for the wrongs his ancestors did by destroying the evil works of their hands and the sin they committed against the Lord. A flame for God's justice was burning within him, and such commitment was pleasing and acceptable to God (2 Kings 23:4-25). King Josiah lived in a time of great spiritual wickedness and the lifestyles and rejections of Christ in our time are likewise vile and perverse, so there is a need for people of Josiah's caliber today. There is a need for men and women of courage to arise today with the light of the Holy Gospel and truth, and proclaim the coming of the Lord Jesus Christ.

In concluding this chapter, we encourage you, as fellow servants of God, not to allow the ungodly talk of the faithless to consume your courage. Instead, use your faith to draw courage from God, since He said in Scripture *"...And I am with you always, to the very end of the age"* (Matthew 28:20 NIV). We, therefore, say Amen to His wonderful promises and unfathomable ability. How do your faith and courage measure up? Is your faith like that of Joshua, Caleb, and Josiah, focusing on the Lord as your strength and courage?

CHAPTER 8

Spirit of Fear

"For God has not given us a spirit of fear, but of power and of love and of a sound mind (2 Timothy 1:7 NKJV).
"For you did not receive the spirit of bondage again to fear, but you received the Spirit of adoption by whom we cry out, "Abba, Father."
(Romans 8:15 NKJV).

Fear is an unpleasant emotion, which is often caused by an internal or external threat such as pain, danger, or harm. Being fearful is closely related to timidity—feeling or showing a lack of courage, confidence, boldness, or determination. Fear displays when we face uncertainty, which leads us to worry how the outcome could affect us.

In this chapter, we examine some situations, and events recorded in the Bible on fear and uncertainty, and how some brave men and women displayed their faith and courage to overcome. This is an important message from the Lord, and we will rely on the Bible for guidance. But first, we will share some short visions from the Lord to help us convey this message effectively.

Visions of Having Faith against Fear

The Lord gave me two simple visions with the central message that we should never run in fear from the enemy when we have received God's forgiveness (Romans 8:1) and perfect love (1 John 4:18). We should also not allow fear to torment us, but should take a stand of courage in Jesus' name. As believers in Christ, we must face all the struggles and storms of life by faith, because He is standing by ready to rescue us (Hebrews 13:5).

Vision Given to Brother Glenn on March 11, 2015

In this vision, I saw myself being carried in the spirit to a town that I have never been to before. As far as I could see, there were people fighting, and everyone had bloodstains on them. Everywhere I looked, I saw people fighting and killing one another. While I walked about observing these violent scenes, a man noticed my presence and started charging towards me. The spirit of fear, which I sensed in that place, gripped my heart. I immediately started running for my life as I was being pursued by the man. As I progressed, I noticed that the man was closing in on me and as my flight path suddenly changed. From what I noticed, I was granted the ability to run in the clouds! Instead of begging for my life when the unknown man was just about to strike me, I yelled in a loud voice, "Hallelujah! Hallelujah! If I have been forgiven, why should I fear?" After uttering these words, my pursuer stopped, and I felt a mighty wind blowing, with the Lord appearing in the clouds dressed in white and disappearing again. As the gentle wind continued to blow, I stopped running and stood firmly facing my enemy. As he got closer to me, he disappeared and then appeared briefly before finally vanishing completely. A great joy filled my heart, leaving me weeping in excitement because of overcoming my fear.

Vision Given to Brother Glenn on March 22, 2015

In this vision, I saw a note floating in midair with the words, "Spirit of Fear." Along with the note, I was shown a scary-looking demon, and I knew that the Lord was telling me not to be fearful of this creature despite its dark and frightening appearance.

Forbidden Weapons of Warfare Against the Fears of Life

Every day, life presents a variety of dangers that bring fear and, sadly, most Christians use ungodly weapons to survive, cope with, or overcome some of these dangers. When people are confronted with fear, they often turn to lying, giving excuses, ignorance, denial, and some other deceitful ways to 'wave off' the immediate threats. For example, when you are regularly late for work or school, do you make fabricated excuses to explain your tardiness to escape the consequences? Alternatively, do you simply say, "Sorry, I'm late again!" without giving a valid excuse? Or do you tell the truth, even though this might provoke immediate action against you? It is natural to succumb to the temptation to lie to fight the fear of punishment. Lying comes from Satan, *"a liar and the father of lies"* (John 8:44).

Whom Should We Fear?

The most common fears we are familiar with, and that others may inflict on us include hurt, insults, embarrassment, humiliation, ridicule, mockery, exclusion, rejection, denial or being denied things. However, succumbing to these fears and the craving to please others or receive their acceptance, validation, and praise are not from the Lord. The Bible encourages us:

- *"The fear of man brings a snare, but whoever trusts in the Lord shall be safe"* (Proverbs 29:25 NKJV).
- *"I, even I, am He who comforts you. Who are you that you should be afraid of a man who will die, and of the son of man who will be made like grass ..."* (Isaiah 51:12 NKJV).
- *"You shall not show partiality in judgment; you shall hear the small as well as the great; you shall not be afraid in any man's presence, for the judgment is God's..."* (Deuteronomy 1:17 NKJV).
- *"And I say to you, my friends, do not be afraid of those who kill the body, and after that have no more that they can do"* (Luke 12:4 NKJV).

In the Bible, we are repeatedly encouraged not to fear man, but to fear God alone. That is, to have reverence for Him, to respect Him, honor Him, obey Him, submit to His authority and discipline, and to worship Him. We should not fear anything or anyone else!

- *"Fear the Lord your God, serve Him only and take your oaths in His name"* (Deuteronomy 6:13 NIV).

- *"You shall fear the Lord your God; you shall serve Him, and to Him you shall hold fast, and take oaths in His name"* (Deuteronomy 10:20 NKJV).

- *"... learn to fear the Lord your God and carefully observe all the words of this law, ...that their children ... may hear and learn to fear the Lord your God as long as you live ..."* (Deuteronomy 31:12-13 NKJV).

- *"... that all the peoples of the earth may know the hand of the Lord, that it is mighty, that you may fear the Lord your God forever"* (Joshua 4:24 NKJV).

- *"Now therefore, fear the Lord, serve Him in sincerity and in truth, and put away the gods which your fathers served on the other side of the River and in Egypt. Serve the Lord!"* (Joshua 24:14 NKJV).

- *"Only fear the Lord, and serve Him in truth with all your heart; for consider what great things He has done for you"* (1 Samuel 12:24 NKJV).

- *"The angel of the Lord encamps all around those who fear Him, and delivers them. Oh, taste and see that the Lord is good; Blessed is the man who trusts in Him! Oh, fear the Lord, you His saints! There is no want to those who fear Him* (Psalm 34:7-9 NKJV).

- *"And do not fear those who kill the body but cannot kill the soul. But rather fear Him who is able to destroy both soul and body in hell"* (Matthew 10:28 NKJV).

- *But I will show you whom you should fear: Fear Him who, after He has killed, has power to cast into hell; yes, I say to you, fear Him! (Luke 12:5 NKJV).*

- *"...Fear God and give glory to Him, for the hour of His judgment has come; and worship Him who made heaven and earth, the sea and springs of water"* (Revelation 14:7 NKJV).

Why is it important to fear God? Because the fear of the Lord equips us with knowledge, instruction, and wisdom (Proverbs 1:7; 15:33). It further helps us to overcome the schemes of the enemy, especially in these last days, and have a close relationship with God, as well as prepare us for heaven.

Biblical Examples of Overcoming Fear

Fear often leads us to willful sinning (Genesis 18:15), the denial of our faith in Jesus Christ or not testifying of our faith especially when under pressure (John 9:22; 12:42). Even Peter and Barnabas fell to fear when they began to withdraw from the Gentiles for fear of the Jews, but Paul powerfully rebuked and corrected them (Galatians 2:12-21).

Our Lord Jesus, knowing that death was fast approaching, wept before our Heavenly Father while fervently resisting the spirit of fear and death, not allowing it to overwhelm Him. Even though the Lord Jesus was tempted just as we are, He set an example for us not to give in to fear (Matthew 26:38-45; Hebrews 4:15). If you recall, Moses the man of God fled from Egypt to Midian because of his fear of Pharaoh after he killed an Egyptian man (Exodus 2:14-15). After being convinced by God's power, Moses put his faith in God and obediently returned to Egypt, defying his fear (Exodus 3:7-17; 4:1-21). Therefore, Moses' fear of man disappeared and his faith rested in God's power (Exodus 20:20).

When Paul faced trials and persecutions, he consciously set aside the fear of man and boldly stated, *"What do you mean by weeping and breaking my heart? For I am ready not only to be bound, but also to die at Jerusalem for the name of the Lord Jesus"* (Acts 21:13 NKJV). His faith was unshaken amid death, humiliation, and rejection. Similarly, we are also encouraged by the boldness of Peter and John after initially fleeing when the Lord was arrested; they stood their ground and declared the faith of their conviction in the resurrection and life-giving sacrifice of our Lord Jesus Christ (Mark 14:50; Acts 3:12-16). The gospel of salvation gave them boldness and hope, delivering them from the fear of man and the sting of death (1 Corinthians 15:55).

In like manner, Stephen bravely endured martyrdom, praising the Lord while being stoned, and even forgiving and pleading for those who hated his faith in Christ as he defied death (Acts 7:51-60). This priceless and precious gospel came about by the Blood of the Lamb of God, and the victory of our faith is eternal life (1 Peter 1:9; 1 John 2:25).

In his lifetime, King David confronted many enemies, both from within his family circle and outside. He addressed fear in some of his Psalms, such as: *"The Lord is my light and my salvation; whom shall I fear? The Lord is the strength of my life; of whom shall I be afraid?"* (Psalm 27:1 NKJV). David expressed confidence in the Lord to overcome fear and gain courage and victory over his circumstances. This encouraging message applies to us as well: *"Wait on the Lord; be of good courage, And He shall strengthen your heart; Wait, I say, on the Lord!"* (Psalm 27:14).

Fear of Satan and Demons

Christ came to break the spirit of fear and to give us new freedom: that of truth leading to salvation, for *"... He Himself likewise shared in the same, that through death He might destroy him who had the power of death, that is, the devil, and release those who through fear of death were all their lifetime subject to bondage"* (Hebrews 2:14-15 NKJV). Furthermore, Jesus proclaimed that when we know the truth, the truth makes us free (John 8:32), and when He makes us free, we are free indeed (John 8:36).

Before Christ's death and resurrection, Satan exercised his power over humanity through the fear of death (Hebrews 2:15). However, after the Lord Jesus Christ was manifested in the flesh, He destroyed the works of the devil (1 John 3:8). He stripped the devil and his demons, and freed humanity from every power of the enemy, *"Having disarmed principalities and powers, He made a public spectacle of them, triumphing over them in it"* (Colossians 2:15). What the forces of darkness were left with as 'strength' is just to induce guilt, fear, and terror causing *"...tribulation, or distress, or persecution, or famine, or nakedness, or peril, or sword..."* (Romans 8:35-36 NKJV). And to *"throw some of you into prison that you may be tested, and you will have tribulation..."* (Revelation 2:10 NKJV). Even so, *"in all these things we are more than conquerors through Him who loved us"* (Romans 8:37 NKJV). The Lord Jesus Christ encourages us not to be afraid, but to *"be faithful until death, and I will give you the crown of life"* (Revelation 2:10b NKJV).

The Lord, knowing that the devil would use fear to control and subdue the human soul, gave us faith and power over all the works of the enemy (Luke 10:19), without which we must endure the torment of fear (1 John 4:18). That is why through the ages those who do not know Christ use death to control and demand obedience. Satan uses some religious sects today to threaten and kill those who accept, believe and follow Jesus Christ as their Lord and Savior. This very same enemy, the fear of death, was challenged and overcome by true soldiers of faith and followers of Christ (Daniel 3:16; Hebrews 11:35-40).

My fellow believer in Christ, do not be deceived! As a Biblical command, we need discernment through the Word of God and the Holy Spirit. Additionally, there are some believers who are busy fighting demons day and night, without much rest in the name of spiritual warfare, and they are using all kinds of strange powers and "supernatural" weapons that the Bible does not even mention (please refer to articles on our website challenging some of these false teachings). The Bible encourages us to magnify and exalt the Lord (Psalm 18:46; 34:3; 97:9). Being involved in these kinds of 'warfare' where Satan and demons are clearly being magnified causes one to be in a state of constant fear. According to this 'new' teaching, the demons they 'see' manifest in the real world, during prayer times, at night, during sleeping time, or even in dreams. The Bible says the Lord gives sound sleep and rest to His beloved (Psalm 127:2; Matthew 11:28).

The Lord Jesus has *"delivered us from the power of darkness and conveyed us into the kingdom of the Son of His love, in whom we have redemption through His blood, the forgiveness of sins"* (Colossians 1:13-14 NKJV). The Lord has also given us *"authority to trample on serpents and scorpions, and over all the power of the enemy..."* (Luke 10:19 NKJV). Instead of fearing Satan, we should, *"Therefore submit to God. Resist the devil and he will flee from you"* (James 4:7 NKJV).

Fear of Man

The Bible sheds light on some instances where people sinned as a result of fearing man. King Saul, for example, disobeyed God's command when he spared the king of the Amalekites. Saul's excuse was that he *"feared the people and obeyed their voice"* (1 Samuel 15:24 NKJV). The Prophet Jeremiah also gave King Zedekiah sound advice, but the king feared his people (Jeremiah 38:17-19). This fear eventually led him to disobey the prophet's words and rebel against King Nebuchadnezzar, and he was subsequently captured, tortured, and died in prison (Jeremiah 52:8-11).

We encourage Christians not to succumb to the fear of man or Satan. In referring to the fear of man, however, we are certainly not encouraging any lawlessness or disrespectful behavior. The values of decency and respect that we learn from the Scriptures restrain us from wicked manners (1 Peter 2:17). You should not embrace the fear or shame of being rejected, ridiculed, punished, or insulted by others because of your submission to our blessed Savior Jesus Christ, or because of the way you look, live, or behave in obedience to Christ.

The fear of fellow man has driven many Christians underground. Sadly, some of these fearful Christians only resurface when they hear the voices of the fearless believers combating the spirits of doubt and faithlessness. Personally, I know of countless Christians who are ashamed of the Gospel because they fear what others might think and say when they find out about their association with Christ. The Lord has done nothing embarrassing or shameful for us to be ashamed about! Brethren, let me encourage you that the Lord did a most noble and humbling act, sacrificing His life and leaving His glory to grant us an eternal destiny, and this is worth celebrating and shouting HALLELUJAH! The whole universe should hear and participate in our celebration! (Revelation 5:9-13). The fear of man is not an option for us; Jesus warned that if we do not confess Him before men, He will not confess us before our Father in heaven (Matthew 10:32-33).

Encouragement to Overcome Fear

Christians should resist the tormenting spirit of fear in Jesus' name and pick up the shield of faith to destroy the insults, shame, and arrows of doubt that Satan uses to smother the spread of the gospel (Ephesians 6:16). *"You are of God, little children, and have overcome them, because He who is in you is greater than he who is in the world"* (1 John 4:4 NKJV).

Through various messages, the Lord has encouraged many brethren not to fear the devil, any human being, or any circumstances. In some cases, we have witnessed how fear has led some people to make desperate and defeated decisions, which resulted in some of them losing their jobs, houses, families, and spouses. The common enemy is fear, fueled by a false faith. Let me counsel you: if your faith is motivated by fear, love is absent, and so is God. The move of fear that you take will fail you and lead to your embarrassment. However, faith is pure and guilt-free, and to know if it is real we should sense and experience joy and peace, not fear (1 John 4:18; Philippians 4:7). Satan can never give us true joy or peace; those fruits are only found in the Lord (Galatians 5:22). The devil is an evil spirit; therefore, anger, hatefulness, and unforgiveness are his trademarks (Revelation 12:12). The will of God is not burdensome; it relieves the yoke and truly frees us! (Matthew 11:26; 1 John 5:3).

So, why are you allowing fear and anxiety to yoke you? Shake it off and walk in your Heavenly victory! (Ephesians 2:6). Remember: *"God has not given us a spirit of fear, but of power and of love and of a sound mind"* (2 Timothy 1:7 NKJV). The Lord God is your comforter, strength, and helper, so do not be afraid of man who perishes (Isaiah 41:10, 13; 51:12). Shun evil and fear God alone; He will destroy both the souls and bodies of the wicked in hell! (Proverbs 3:7; Matthew 10:28; Revelation 21:8)

In the next chapter, we will continue addressing the topic of fear. We will also discuss the fear of death, in addition to sharing some testimonies and revelations from the Lord on the subject.

CHAPTER 9

Fear of Death

Since the children have flesh and blood, He too shared in their humanity so
that by His death He might break the power of him who holds the power of
death—that is, the devil—and free those who all their lives were held in
slavery by their fear of death (Hebrews 2:14-15 NIV).

The Bible tell us that our most common fear and the deadliest enemy
is death (1 Corinthians 15:26) and that we are all destined to die once,
and then face judgment (Hebrews 9:27). So, there is no doubt that death
is real. However, talking about physical death without referring to the
Biblical teaching of the Hereafter is, in my opinion, gross negligence and
not telling the whole truth. It is also unwise to deny the reality of death,
which is so vividly described in the Word of God (John 11:25-26; 1
Corinthians 15:55). While science and the world at large offer various
explanations on the hereafter, or lack thereof, we must have confidence
in the revealed truth of God's Word and the testimony given by our
Lord Jesus Christ. He alone died and came back to life (1 Corinthians
15:4). The truth about the life, death, and resurrection of the Lord Jesus
Christ is flawless and trustable (Proverbs 30:5; 1 Corinthians 15:19).
Biblically, death occurs when the body and soul are separated (Matthew
10:28). The body returns to the earth, and the spirit returns to God
(Genesis 3:19; Ecclesiastes 12:7). If the deceased person were born again,
he would be present with the Lord in Heaven (2 Corinthians 5:1-10).
However, if the person were not born again at the time of their physical
death, that soul would have gone to hell (Psalm 9:17; Luke 16:19-31).

As we know, people are facing death every day, and it often happens unexpectedly and without warning. It comes upon us like a thief (Luke 12:20). Since we do not know our time of departure from this present life, we should expect it to happen any moment. Therefore, we should always be ready and prepared. Readiness for death is best expected and celebrated if we wait for it in Christ (Philippians 1:21).

During one of our witnessing rounds a few years ago, I was sharing the gospel with a few young men when one of them interrupted me and lividly voiced his opposition, telling me that what I talked about could not be true since I had never seen the Lord Jesus, nor did I know if there was life after death. These are points that unbelievers may throw at Christians to challenge their faith. I calmly explained to him that the message of the Bible is to be received by faith, and if it is not taken by faith, then we would have no hope (Hebrews 10:23). Furthermore, I also shared with them that I am convinced that Christ is real and that there is life after death. I also shared some of my own experiences with the Lord and a near death experience I had when I developed breathing problems after overdosing on marijuana back in the early 1990s after I had returned to my worldly ways. After sharing my testimony with them, he could not advance his argument, so he began attacking the Bible. At that point, I just blessed him and encouraged him to read the tract. Many people nowadays express similar skepticism as this young man. Generally, in today's society people often use history to either deny or justify some decisions, especially when this relates to things that affected their current situations, such as major political events, world wars, etc. However, those who believe and appreciate the values of history while denying the historical significance, values and message of the Bible, are denying themselves the free gift of salvation and Heaven.

In the Holy Scriptures, and at the heart of the Christian message, we are told of the gift of salvation and God's promise of eternal life (John 3:16-18). The Lord Jesus Christ came to tell all humanity that our death is certain, but he reassures us:" I *have come that they may have life, and that they may have it more abundantly"* (John 10:10 NIV). How can we have this abundant life? Only if we believe and accept God's gift (John 3:3-18).

Man's Sin Leading to Death

We would like to acknowledge that many scholars and ministers of the Gospel before us have thoroughly studied and presented the subject on the fall of man from God's grace. However, for the benefit of those who might never have read this account of the fall of man or understood its significance from a Biblical perspective, we briefly relate it here.

In the Bible record of the temptation and fall of man (Genesis 3:1-24), God commanded Adam and Eve, our first ancestors, not to eat from the tree of knowledge of good and evil. In other words, man had the choice to obey or to reject this command and suffer the consequences (Genesis 2:17). After submitting to Satan's advances, they ate from the forbidden tree (Genesis 3:4-6). As a result, Adam and Eve lost their innocence before the Lord God, and immediately guilt and shame plagued their conscience (Genesis 3:7-11). Before they ate from the tree, Adam and Eve had enjoyed a perfect, peaceful, and conflict-free life with the Lord God; they had been guilt-free, carefree, and fearless (Genesis 2:15-25). As it was, after the fall guilt, shame, and fear possessed the entire human race until One from above came who was sinless, guilt-free, and fearless to take away our guilt and restore us to God's anger (2 Corinthians 5:21; Isaiah 53:4; John 1:29; 3:31). The Bible tells us that *"the gift is not like the trespass. For if the many died by the trespass of the one man, how much more did God's grace and the gift that came by the grace of the one man, Jesus Christ, overflow to the many"* (Romans 5:15 NIV).

Consequently, man's violation of God's law led to death, and God's solution was peace through Jesus Christ (Romans 6:23). Through Christ, our fear of death has been absolved (John 11:25); this is the hope of all Christians who walk in fear of God daily.

The Lord's Confirmation that there is Life after Death

Before we share the Lord's message and some visions relating to this subject, kindly allow me to give a brief background. You would also appreciate that it is necessary to share this testimony so that you will understand why the Lord gave us messages and visions regarding one of my aunts. In February 2015, my family and I attended the funeral of one of my beloved aunts who passed away in late January 2015. I enjoyed a very close relationship with her as she was like a mother to me. Due to my own mother's ill health and my father being in prison when I was young, she took care of my sisters and me. Her passing came as no surprise as she was bedridden for about four months, and she died after suffering a stroke, along with many other internal complications. It is not a good memory to recall, but weeks before her death my aunt literally wasted away and screamed daily for help because of the pain she endured. The stroke she suffered robbed her of her speech, but we could still understand some of her murmurings, especially when she called some of us by name.

When my family visited her on December 30, 2014, I asked her if I should pray for her healing. To my surprise, she responded by raising her right arm towards the roof while rolling her eyes upwards indicating to us that she preferred to die. In the hearing of all who were present, I replied to her that God determines life and death and that I could not pray for such a request. At that point, I asked her if she wanted to accept the Lord in her life. She declined, indicating "No" by moving her head sideways. I proceeded to pray for her anyway and I asked the Lord to help her in whichever way since He knew her heart and needs. A few days later, I received a Word from the Lord during prayer that she did not have faith in Him (Hebrews 11:6). In our zeal to get her to accept the Lord a few months before her death, we encouraged her to repent and to forgive those who had wronged her and to start growing her faith by reading her Bible and abstain from alcohol consumption. It is important to know that God gives perfect peace to those who trust in

Him (Isaiah 26:3), but there is no peace or rest for the wicked (Isaiah 48:22). During my aunt's excessive screaming and her calling of some deceased people for help, we knew she did not have peace. About eight days after we had visited her, I received a vision from the Lord on January 7, 2015. In this vision, I was standing in front of her house and facing her front door with many other people who were gathered to listen to a preaching. I could not hear what was being said, but I knew we were gathering for her funeral, and I heard the Lord saying: *"My daughter Joyce (not real name) is no longer in this life."* As confirmation, the Lord gave my daughter, Jaydeen, a vision that same morning in which she saw my aunt in a coffin at the graveyard.

You would have noticed that the Lord did not say she was dead but that *"she was no longer in this life,"* simply meaning that she was absent here and that she has gone to another life. A few days after we had these visions, I called my aunt Joyce and her granddaughter on the phone and informed them of our visions. Now, since she was speechless and unable to answer the phone herself, her granddaughter helped her. My aunt could understand what I was saying on the phone as I could hear her bitterly crying and sobbing. Brethren, it is important to note that every person who is alive still has an opportunity to repent and go to Heaven (Ezekiel 18:32). Being overcome with grief myself, I comforted her that the Lord was on the other side (Heaven) waiting for her and that she need not fear death, but that she must repent of her sins. I also reiterated that she forgives those who had wronged her (Matthew 6:12; Luke 6:37). By her calling of people's names with an angry face, we knew that she had unforgiveness against some people whom we knew owed her some money. In fulfillment of our visions exactly twenty-one days later, we received word that she had died and gone to the other life.

Because this message is important, we wanted to share this testimony with everybody in accordance with the Lord's will. So we all prayed and fasted for three days as a family and ministry and continued praying for over two weeks. After our praying regarding her eternal destiny, we asked the Lord which side of the afterlife my aunt went to

(Heaven or Hell). On the morning of February 16, 2015, around 5:00 AM, I received an answer to this prayer, and this is what the Lord revealed in a short vision.

Vision of My Aunt's Eternal Destiny

Given to Brother Glenn on February 16, 2015, around 5:00 AM

"I found myself standing in a very dim and untidy room with clothes and other things strewn all around. Suddenly, my deceased aunt entered the room shabbily dressed and calling me in Afrikaans, using my nickname as was her custom, "B...Kom, kom ek wil ook nou Bybel lees" (Come, come I also want to start reading the Bible now). As she said that, fear gripped my heart, and I was afraid to even get closer to her. However, by some unknown force I was drawn closer to her, and as she passed by me there was a very strong and foul stench like that of a badly decomposed body or something similar; it was an awful, disgusting odor! (Isaiah 3:24). Upon her request to start reading Bible, I bent down to reach for a cardboard box, which was in front of me, looking for a Bible to give her. After searching through the various items lying all around, I came across a Bible with a black cover, but I could not reach her or get closer to her. I could only hear her screaming somewhere in the dark, and I knew her rejection of the Lord meant that she went to outer darkness (Matthew 25:30)."

Since she is my very own aunt whom I regarded as a mother, and a person who took care of me, loved me and disciplined me, it would have been hard for any person to share such a shameful and painful testimony about her. However, the Lord has allowed us to see, hear and feel some of her sufferings, and to warn you of the fate that awaits all unrepentant sinners. Furthermore, what we can learn from this vision is that everyone who dies without repenting of their sins, including mockers, unbelievers, and worldly Christians, will end up in hell! While the Lord did not show me that she was literally in the flames of Hell, the vision above is confirmation that she did not go to Heaven. She wanted to make right with God by repenting and reading the Bible only on the other side of this life, however, it was forever too late. Weeks before she died, and in a desperate attempt to get her saved, I prayed every day for her deliverance, healing, and salvation; from the time I first heard of her stroke and cancer that she suffered internally, right until the morning we received news of her passing. In truth, God gives grace to those who ask and call upon Him for help. The Bible clearly reminds us:

"For He is our God, and we are the people of His pasture, and the sheep of His hand. Today, if you will hear His voice: "Do not harden your hearts, as in the rebellion, as in the day of trial in the wilderness" (Psalm 95:7-8; Hebrews 3:7-15 NKJV).

Below we are sharing another vision from the Lord regarding a friend who did not accept the Lord Jesus Christ and repent of his sins.

Vision of a Man Who Died in His Sins

Vision Given to Brother Glenn on May 11, 2016

On the morning of May 11, 2016, I had a short vision of a friend who died a few years ago in a car accident. Although I could not see his face, I could still recognize him. To me, it felt as if I went to pay him a visit., The place where he was appeared to be foggy and very dark, but I could see his figure as I knew him. When I looked at him, I saw the sins he had committed while here on earth, and I knew immediately that he died in his sins. Being accompanied by someone, I said to my companion, "Can we not help him out of here so that he may be resurrected with the righteous?" (Luke14:14). After those words had left my mouth I was interrupted, and I heard a voice saying, *"It is appointed unto all men to die once and thereafter to face judgment"* (Hebrews 9:27). I knew that there was nothing more we could do for the young man and the vision ended.

In this vision, the Lord was confirming that there will be a resurrection of the righteous and a resurrection of the wicked (John 5:28-29; Acts 24:15). From the Bible, it is clear that there's nothing that anybody can do to help those who died in their sins or help them make right with God and be part of the resurrection of the righteous (Ezekiel

18:20; John 8:24; Luke 16:26). In the light of this warning from the Lord, we encourage you not to be deceived by thinking you will have another opportunity at salvation after the curtain of this life has closed on you. If you die in your sins and without Christ, you will rise again but only to be condemned (Daniel 12:2). Fear the Lord and seek Him while you are in this life. This warning is for your salvation (Isaiah 55:6).

Jesus Christ, Our Risen Savior, Our Hope

The Lord Jesus Christ is our eternal hope, *"...who has destroyed death and has brought life and immortality to light through the gospel"* (2 Timothy 1:10 NIV). Today, many people deny the resurrection of the dead and the coming judgment. We know that this kind of thinking is not new, and indeed even in the days of Paul, there were such people (1 Corinthians 15:12). In response to them, Paul boldly asserted:

"But if there is no resurrection of the dead, then Christ is not risen. And if Christ is not risen, then our preaching is empty and your faith is also empty. Yes, and we are found false witnesses of God, because we have testified of God that He raised up Christ, whom He did not raise up—if in fact the dead do not rise. For if the dead do not rise, then Christ is not risen. And if Christ is not risen, your faith is futile; you are still in your sins! Then also those who have fallen asleep in Christ have perished. If in this life only we have hope in Christ, we are of all men the most pitiable" (1 Corinthians 15:13-19 NKJV).

In Christ, not only will we be alive after death, but death itself will be destroyed (1 Corinthians 15:22, 26) and be cast eternally into the lake of fire (Revelation 20:14). As a faithful promise, once death has been destroyed forever, the Lord will comfort His chosen people and remove all our shame, reproach, and disgrace we ever suffered for His name (Isaiah 25:8)—*"And God will wipe away every tear from their eyes; there shall be no more death, nor sorrow, nor crying. There shall be no more pain, for the former things have passed away"* (Revelation 21:4 NKJV).

Avoiding Eternal Death

The Bible's message about victory over death through Christ Jesus is not fictional; it is real! (1 Corinthians 15:56-57). Your fear of death could be turned into joy if you believe and accept God's gift and Christ's victory over death. Through Christ, we are free from the law of sin and death (Romans 8:2). Without the Lord Jesus, whom both the Bible and some historical accounts acknowledge as having died and rose again (1 Corinthians 15:6), we would have every reason to fear death. However, in Him, we believe in the hope of someday receiving eternal life. He took our guilt, and we know guilt stimulates fear, and that fear relates to punishment (1 John 4:18). The fear of the Lord and the Word of God is a well of life, keeping us from death and saving us from its trap (Proverbs 13:14; 14:27). As we seek and follow the Lord faithfully, the Bible gives us hope and sure promises we can look forward to:

> *He will swallow up death forever. The Sovereign Lord will wipe away the tears from all faces; He will remove His people's disgrace from all the earth. The Lord has spoken. In that day they will say, "Surely this is our God; we trusted in Him, and He saved us. This is the Lord, we trusted in him; let us rejoice and be glad in His salvation"* (Isaiah 25:8-9 NIV).

> *When the perishable has been clothed with the imperishable, and the mortal with immortality, then the saying that is written will come true: "Death has been swallowed up in victory"* (1 Corinthians 15:54 NIV).

Are you still afraid of death? Are you living a life of holiness, partaking of the heavenly calling (Hebrews 3:1), and walking on the narrow path that leads to everlasting life? (Matthew 7:14). Or, are you among the many who embrace friendship with the world (James 4:4) and are walking on the wide highway that leads to destruction? (Matthew 7:13). Be rest assured that "*...the hour is coming in which all who are in the graves will hear His voice and come forth—those who* *have done good, to the resurrection of life, and those who have done evil, to the resurrection of condemnation"* (John 5:28-29 NKJV).

Vision: The Lord is Coming Soon!

Given to Brother Glenn on February 11, 2015

I was in a large room, which was illuminated by a light similar to a sunset, with members of our congregation. While I could not see the Lord, I knew that He was standing right there. I read to them from a white page with messages from the Lord, which I was not allowed to remember. Again, I was given another message to read, which was written in Afrikaans on a white page. As I read the message the first time it did not make sense. I re-read it two more times over, and it confused me more as the text changed to other words. However, I was able to gain an understanding of that writing after I recalled the vision, and this is what was written, *"The people I have appointed for Heaven must not play with their salvation in this very last hour."* Soon after reading this message to our congregation, it felt as if the Lord could come right at that very moment. At the same time, I could sense the excitement of the brethren present. After reading the message, I also saw a sister who once attended our ministry being in another room. She was saying something, but I could not understand exactly what she was saying. I was made to understand that she was using excuses to justify her lukewarm state.

CHAPTER 10

Salvation Received on Deathbed and Missed Opportunity

"We are confident, yes, well pleased rather to be absent from the body and to be present with the Lord"(2 Corinthians 5:8; Luke 23:43 NKJV).

On June 15, 2013, two of my daughters (Charis and Jaydeen) and I attended my nephew's funeral in my hometown Vryburg, South Africa. My aunt, Joyce (same one mentioned in the previous chapter), requested me to go and pray for one of her sick friends and neighbor, Aunt Lily. I knew Aunt Lily personally as a dear and caring mother whom I last met over thirty years before. When we arrived, my son Johnny and my neighbor's daughter, Shunay, joined us. After entering the house, Aunt Lily's grandson led us to her room. After we had exchanged greetings, we introduced ourselves to her. With a smile on her face, Aunt Lily shook hands with each one of us. She removed the breathing mask and tried speaking to us, but she experienced some breathing problems and started coughing and gulping for air. She put the breathing mask back on, and we encouraged her just to gesture with her hands and nod with her head. We were moved by her condition and illness, so we spoke a few encouraging words in the name of the Lord Jesus Christ. After talking to her, I asked her if she would like to accept Jesus as her Lord and Savior and receive the Lord's free gift of healing. She nodded in agreement, so I asked the children who accompanied me to join me in prayer and faith for her healing. I led her to the Lord in prayer while also praying for her healing in Jesus' name. She surely had faith; immediately after the prayer, she received her speech back, and after she realized this, she removed the breathing mask and spoke to us with ease and without difficulty! When we saw this miracle right in front of us, we greatly rejoiced with her as she shed tears of joy and gave praise to the Lord. After regaining her speech, Aunt Lily explained to us that she was diagnosed with throat cancer and the treatment she had received caused her severe pain and suffering. As she shared her ordeal, we could sense her bitterness towards the doctors and the people who treated her. This led us to encourage her to forgive them, now that she was born again (saved).

We gave her a few of the gospel tracts we had to encourage her, and when we noticed her Bible on her bedside, I told her to read the Word of God for the sustenance of her salvation and healing. We also told her that if she had enough faith, she would experience complete healing, but if not, she should not have any fear of death should the Lord decide to take her home (to Heaven). After further encouragement and before we left, we asked her if we could take a few pictures of her to share our joy with others, and she heartily agreed. After speaking with her, we bid her farewell, and we all left, amazed by what the Lord had done. As we were outside leaving, I was filled with joy in my heart and I hurried back to her bedroom window to shake her hand for the last time. While she was waving us goodbye, I took a final picture of her.

Surprisingly, the following day, June 16, 2013, around 3:00 PM, I received a phone call from my sister informing me that she had just received news that Aunty Lily passed away. Instead of crying, upon hearing this sad news, I rejoiced in the LORD and exclaimed, HALLELUYAH! I did not rejoice because she had died; I loved her, and I rejoiced because she died in peace and in the LORD! (Psalm 116:15). That same evening, before we went to bed Charis, Jaydeen and I prayed in agreement and asked the Lord if He could show us if Aunt Lily made it to Heaven. We give glory to the Lord Jesus Christ for saving her on her death bed! Now, seeing her breathing and speaking without the mask appeared to be a remarkable miracle to us. However, we were even exceedingly joyful that she accepted the

Lord and died in Him. In the vision, which follows below, the Lord Jesus Christ said in a loud voice, *"SHE IS FREE!!!!"* Let us rejoice together for Heaven received a soul (Luke 15:7). The following pictures show her before and after we prayed with for her.

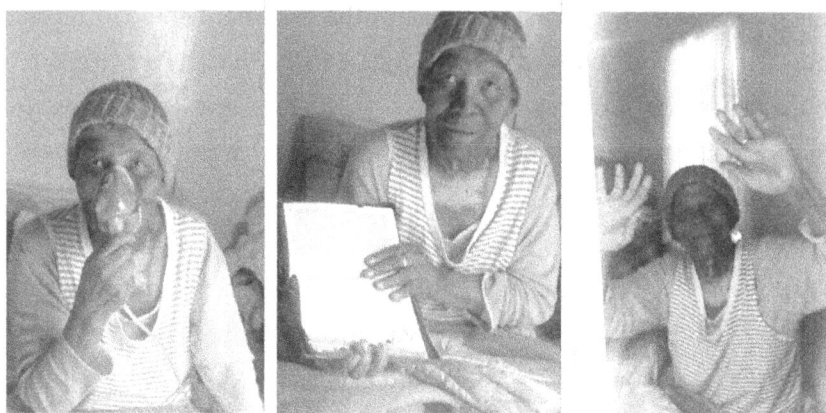

The first picture was taken before we prayed for Aunty Lily. She tried speaking to us, but she choked and coughed because she inhaled too much air. Her voice was husky and frail.

The second picture was taken after praying for her. You can see the burning wounds inflicted by the chemotherapy on her neck. I noticed two Bibles by her bedside, and I told her never to close the Bible. She immediately got hold of one Bible (the Afrikaans one), and while she opened it to read, I told her to start reading from Matthew and pray immediately after we are gone.

The third picture was the final picture I had taken of Aunt Lily before we left. As she was waving, she praised the Lord, and she reached for my hand for a final greeting through the window.

A Vision of a Deceased Woman in Heaven: "She is Free!"

Vision Given to Charis on June 17, 2013

"I had a vision from the Lord this morning. I heard the thunderous voice of the Lord saying, *"Go outside!"* Immediately, I went outside the house, and the CLOUD of the Lord appeared in a dazzling white light with the Lord inside the cloud. I was given a small white umbrella to cover me from the glorious LIGHT and splendor coming from the Lord. Without warning, I was immediately transported into the cloud, and the

Lord and I went up to Heaven. Moments later, I found myself in Heaven. Seconds later, the Lord and the tiny white umbrella disappeared. After the Lord had disappeared, I saw what He wanted to show me. I saw Aunt Lily in Heaven sitting cross-legged on a wooden chair with glass-like supporting pillars. Aunt Lily smilingly waved at me to come over to her, and she said in Afrikaans: "Sê jou pa ek sê dankie dat hy vir my gebid het en my na die Here toe gely het. Die Here wou my heeltemal nie genees het nie, Hy wou my net huis toe [Heaven home] geneem het, soos jou pa gesê het." With a beautiful smile on her face and voice, she continued and said, "Dit is baie aangenaam hier in die Hemel." I replied and said, "Ek sal my pa gaan sê en dit was n plesier van my kant af." **Translation:** *"Go tell your father I say thank you that he prayed for me and led me to the Lord. The Lord did not want to heal me completely, but He wanted to bring me home to Heaven as your father said before he prayed for me. It is very nice up here in Heaven!"* I (Charis) replied and said: *"I will tell him and it is only a pleasure from my side."* After speaking, she showed me the burned scars that had been inflicted on her chest by the chemotherapy were totally gone. Her skin looked very soft, clean and tender like a baby's.

After showing me her new skin, Aunt Lily got up from the chair she was sitting on and she started to turn all around like a little girl rejoicing with so much peace and happiness in her face, and being dressed in a pure white dress with silky white bally-like shoes. What a beautiful sight to behold her joy and the scene playing out before me! I saw pure white lily flowers with her name *Lily* written on the side of the road. She bent down and started picking these Lily flowers and blowing them into the air. She turned around and looked at me smilingly. Moments later, and she jumped up with her hands in the air and as she jumped, she was suspended in the air and I saw a beautiful, golden crown with the name *"LILY"* being placed by the Lord on her head. I then saw a rainbow-shaped banner appearing on her right side in yellow ink: *"SHE IS FREE!"* Being prompted by the Spirit, I uttered my last words to her and I said, "Ek moet nou gaan" ("I must leave now"). She looked at me and smiled, and I returned the smile. Just as I turned around, the vision was over."

As an encouragement, beloved brethren, please do not undermine God, and what He wants to do through you for other people. Go out in obedience, pray for the sick, and preach the gospel to populate Heaven; the second testimony below is a sobering reminder of this.

Vision of Missed Opportunity to Witness to a Lost Soul

Before we share this vision, I would like to give a brief background so that you can understand the context. The person identified in the vision was a homeless man called Jim who lived on the streets until my father offered him a place to stay. When my family and I visited my parents for the holidays in December 2014, we met Jim at my father's house. I exchanged greetings with Uncle Jim one afternoon, and I encouraged him to do something for me which he did. However, it never dawned on me to witness to him. I simply took it for granted that others might have witnessed to him, so I didn't have to. Being a witness of the Gospel, I have always taken every opportunity to witness to all people – young, old, rich and poor, and whichever race irrespective of their social class. Uncle Jim died at age seventy-four and was buried on February 20, 2016. Being soul minded, we are always troubled and wondering if a deceased person made their lives right with the Lord before they passed on. So, Uncle Jim's sudden death was of concern to us. In a surprise vision, the Lord showed Charis his final destiny.

Vision Given to Charis on February 21, 2016

"I had a vision on February 21, 2016, just after our early morning prayers. I saw a very long street and towards the top end and on the right-hand side of the road, there was beautiful and soft looking green grass, and to the left side of the road towards the lower end of the street, the grass was dead and withered. I saw Uncle Jim sitting and having a conversation with a fine looking and beautiful young angel who had the appearance of a young man. I could sense that he was being witnessed to and told that he needed to be saved to get to Heaven or to go over to the greener side. As l got closer to them, I heard the angel saying to him, "Uncle Glenn was the only one who could have helped you get your life right with God, but look he is waiting at the end of the road for you." Immediately, I saw Uncle Jim getting up and he started walking towards my father. I saw my father waving at him from afar and in a desperate attempt, he stretched out his right hand towards my father to help him, but his hand was too short and the distance too wide. When Uncle Jim realized he could not reach or get near to my father, he wept and started crying bitterly in hopelessness as if saying that he couldn't reach my father. By this, I knew it was too late for him to repent. This was the end of the vision."

After hearing this vision, I (Brother Glenn) was greatly disturbed and moved to tears. I regarded this vision as a solemn rebuke from the Lord for undermining and despising the salvation of Uncle Jim. Now, because of my negligence and irreverence, the Lord was rebuking me for missing the opportunity to witness and lead Uncle Jim to Him when I had a chance to do so. This precious soul is now lost for all eternity, and Heaven was denied one soul. After praying and asking for forgiveness, the Lord spoke to my heart saying that every individual soul, irrespective of their social standing, is important to Him and that He died for the salvation of all people. Even as I am sharing here, I am still deeply hurt and regretful with pain only the Lord knows and pain that He experiences when He loses a soul. Many of us despise people of a lower social order especially the homeless, addicts or beggars. However, the Lord will not overlook, for *"A bruised reed he will not break, and a smoldering wick he will not snuff out…"* (Isaiah 42:3 NIV). Therefore, with this message, the Lord is encouraging and warning you as His witnesses never to neglect to share the Gospel with others. He will hold us accountable for the souls we neglect evangelizing to. To witness, you do not need to be a pastor or full-time minister of the gospel to share the Good News! (Ezekiel 33:7-9; Matthew 28:19; Mark 16:15).

CHAPTER 11

Blaming God When Bad Things Happen – Part I

But indeed, O man, who are you to reply against God? Will the thing formed say to him who formed it, "Why have you made me like this?" (Romans 9:20 NKJV)

This chapter is not an attempt to answer life's difficult questions, such as "why do the wicked or worldly people seem to do well?" (Job 21:7; Jeremiah 12:1), nor do we claim to be sitting on God's seat to answer on His behalf (Isaiah 1:18). We do not have all the answers either; instead, we solely rely on the Holy Spirit to teach us and guide us.

Many Christians fail and give up on their faith after allowing sin to eat away at their faith and obedience. The Lord has given this message in response to people, both saved and unsaved, who blame Him for their misfortunes. The principal reason people blame the Lord is based on their understanding that God is all-powerful and He directs all things. So they ask, why does He allow evil to happen to people in general?

As a ministry, we too have our set of problems and challenges, even though the Lord was speaking to us the way He did. He still expects us to pray and have faith in Him if bad things trap us. Sitting around and blaming Him only gives rise to more trouble! Complaining against God and blaming Him cost countless Israelites their lives (Numbers 14:29). Therefore, in our sufferings, we accept the discomfort of the situations we are facing, while we trust the Lord for complete deliverance as we continue to develop the fruit of perseverance and longsuffering (2 Timothy 3:10-11).

Why Do People Blame God?

The Scriptures record some instances where people directly blamed the Lord for their unfortunate situations. Naomi, the widow of Elimelech, was one such person who became bitter after losing her husband and two sons. She said, *"…my daughters. It is more bitter for me than for you, because the Lord's hand has turned against me!"* (Ruth 1:13 NIV). She also said, *"Don't call me Naomi' she told them. 'Call me Mara, because the Almighty has made my life very bitter. I went away full, but the Lord has brought me back empty. Why call me Naomi? The Lord has afflicted me; the Almighty has brought misfortune upon me'"* (Ruth 1:20-21 NIV).

Furthermore, when tragedy struck Job, he said, *"Naked I came from my mother's womb, and naked I will depart. The Lord gave and the Lord has taken away; may the name of the Lord be praised."* (Job 1:21 NIV). Equally, after discovering he was in trouble, Adam blamed God saying *"the woman You put here with me…"* (Genesis 3:12 NIV).

Similarly, Moses blamed God for sending him to Pharaoh, given the harsh treatment Pharaoh and his officials meted out on the Israelites (Exodus 5:22-23). In these few Scriptures, we see two undeniable facts, namely: God is present and has a direct interest in the suffering of the people, and that He wants to save them. Knowing God's fearful power, the affected individual's questioned why He allowed the unfortunate situations to happen.

As humans, our immediate response to an unfortunate situation is, "where is God and why did He allow this to happen to me?" We should remember the Bible says that a day of evil is reserved for all humankind (Ecclesiastes 9:2-3; Job 14:1; Acts 20:24). The world, as we know it, is filled with every kind of evil all around. You probably may have heard people arguing that God is the author of all the confusion and evil in the world since He created everything (1 Corinthians 14:33). We do know that all things are from God (Psalm 24:1; 50:12) and that He is almighty. However, God does not bring evil (James 1:13; Romans 1:30). Evil is executed upon us under the direct influence of Satan to cause us harm (Genesis 50:20; 1 Peter 5:8-9). It is utterly wicked and blasphemous to blame God when evil traps us. Shall God, who warns us to "abstain from every form of evil" (1 Thessalonians 5:22 NKJV), still bring evil upon us? I consider God to be fair, peaceful and righteous. If we claim that He purposely brought evil upon us, would He have a basis to judge the guilty if He was the author of such evil? (2 Thessalonians 1:5-8; 2:5-8; Proverbs 11:21). Therefore, if the Scriptures declare that our sin reveals God's righteousness (Romans 3:5-8), can we still blame Him when bad things happen to us? Of course, not! The Lord God will punish those who are responsible for the evil against us! (2 Thessalonians 1:6).

Scripturally, we can conclude that God created everything, except evil, for evil is an act of rebellion against God (sin or wickedness). The Bible tells us that He created *"...the tree of life [which] was also in the midst of the garden, and the tree of the knowledge of good and evil"* (Genesis 2:9 NKJV). God gave man free will and choice to eat from every tree in the garden, but He commanded him not to eat from the tree of the knowledge of good and evil; violation of this command would lead to man's death (Genesis 2:17). We know that death and evil entered the world when man disobeyed this command (Genesis 3:6; 16-19). In His great love for man, God gave man commands to live by, choices and consequences that lead to eternal life or death, blessing or disaster. He pleads with us to *"choose life that both you and your descendants may live"* (Deuteronomy 30:19-20 NKJV). Some might find the Scripture in Isaiah 45:7 as implying that God created evil, but we know evil was allowed to co-exist with good in the world so that man may choose good and life. The word "evil" as used in the Bible is derived from a Hebrew word that means "adversity, affliction, disaster, calamity, distress, misery" – these are the consequences God allows to come upon us a result of our rebellion against His Word and commands (Jeremiah 32:23). If God were the author of evil, He would not have given us commands to live by to root out evil; would He? (Luke 11:28; Deuteronomy 11:13). Being a just and holy God, He thus separates Himself from sinful behavior—He is light and in Him is no darkness at all (1 John 1:5). Therefore, blaming God when people's negligence and sinful behavior cause them harm, or when bad things happen, is being wicked, foolish and faithless. Job reacted in a dignified way, and he rather praised God despite his predicament (Job 1:20-21). Also, Satan asked for permission from God to make job's life miserable. The devil used all kinds of evil devices, causing death, suffering, and devastation (Job 1:1-22; 2:1-10). Satan used evil, but God preserved and rebuilt Job's life and fully restored everything to him (Job 42:12-17). During King David's forty-year reign, he had many difficulties, and he wrote many of his Psalms when he was in great distress. Instead of blaming God, he chose to humble himself and trust Him, finding comfort in God's goodness and praising Him despite the dire circumstances he was going through. In the end, he was blessed as the Scripture declares, and *"he died at a good old age, having enjoyed long life, wealth and honor"* (1 Chronicles 29:26-28 NIV).

Is There Evil in the World?

Without going into complex theological questions and debates, the Bible asserts that after the fall of man, evil became part of our human nature and bad things followed because of that condition (Genesis 3:1-19; 6:5). As human beings, we conveniently only blame God when things are going against us, but when things are going well with us, we express our satisfaction through indulgent appreciation. In other words, we only accept the good, and we even thank God for our good lives. We receive God's blessings without complaining, and celebrate these as "good fortunes" or "good luck. The truth is, after the fall, God allowed (through our choice, as Adam and Eve did) evil into this world to exist alongside us so that in our distress we should wait for and long for His grace and deliverance (Genesis 3:22-24; 2 Corinthians 1:1-11). What many of us fail to realize is that humans share this planet with Satan and demonic spirits who come and go as they please (Job 2:2; 1 Peter 5:8). Satan also uses people, nature, and his evil powers to cause harm to people as he did against Job (Job 1:13-19; 2:1-9). In the New Testament, Satan also made a similar request to destroy Peter, but an intercessory prayer from the Lord Jesus rendered the devil's evil plans useless (Luke 22:31).

The Bible clearly warns the inhabitants of the earth that Satan has come to the earth to steal, kill and destroy souls (John 10:10; Revelation 12:12). This prophetic passage is an account of what happened in the heavens at the fall of Satan; he was hurled down to the earth together with his demonic host (Luke 10:18; Revelation 12:9). His work is to deceive and give God a bad name so that he can "cash in" on people's souls. However, evil is decreed to operate on this earth until the final consummation (Matthew 13:27-30). Therefore, watch out people! Evil is all around us! Our relief and protection against the unseen evil are in Jesus Christ alone. He is our only hiding place! (Genesis 4:7; Proverbs 18:10; Colossians 1:15-20).

As it is, God saw the evil that man brought upon himself through disobedience (Romans 5:12-21), so He gave us the Lord Jesus Christ to rescue us from the effects of sin and all the evil resulting from this. The Lord God came with a message, saying that He loved the world and wanted to save humanity from the coming evil (wages of sin) through the suffering, death, and resurrection of our Lord Jesus Christ (Matthew 3:7; John 3:16-18). By accepting Christ, we become children of God (John 1:12-13; 1 John 3:1) and are guaranteed victory—a complete escape from all harm and evil, and lasting peace for the hereafter (Psalm 37:37; Isaiah 57:2; Matthew 25:21). In this current age, however, we will have trouble, for the nature of evil is kindled and directed against all humankind. The Good News is that we have an escape and a Source of comfort and hope in the Lord (John 16:33; Romans 15:13; 2 Thessalonians 3:16).

Warning of Pending Trouble

In a short message a few years ago, the Lord warned a sister that trouble was decreed against her and that she must "*WATCH OUT for wicked people.*" In three separate messages, the Lord warned her saying that Satan was using wicked people to destroy her life. Sadly, she disregarded the Lord's warnings. Consequently, evil trapped her and this led her into sin. These warnings are reminiscent of some trouble that was decreed against Paul. However, he did not panic and sin, and his suffering glorified God (Acts 21:11).

In a separate incident, my wife lost her cell phone and, in comforting her, the Lord said that she had ignored the Holy Spirit who had warned her to guard her phone. Because of ignoring the Holy Spirit, her phone was stolen, and that theft did not escape the Lord's eyes; He promised to punish the person who stole the phone.

If we are constantly in prayer and have faith, the Lord will warn us of looming dangers. Otherwise, if we are not vigilant in prayer and are negligent and sinful, we'll be trapped by evil (Luke 21:36). As a discouragement against habitual sinful desires, we should realize that evil will catch up with us. Sin pays generous wages! (Romans 6:23). When we sin, we receive the compensation for evil because we failed to heed the warning.

We may earn evil because of our actions and our failure to heed the Lord's warnings. In the Bible, we see the following examples:

- The Lord allowed an evil Spirit to torment Saul (1 Samuel 19:9).

- David was promised calamity after his extramarital affair with Bathsheba and subsequent murder of her husband Uriah (2 Samuel 12:9-14).

- After Solomon had sinned, God raised up adversaries against him (1 Kings 11:14-25).

- Some people were also struck with leprosy as in the case of Miriam when she spoke against Moses (Numbers 12:10) and King Uzziah who sinned in the temple of the Lord by trying to burn incense (2 Chronicles 26:20).

- King Josiah, though a righteous man, died in battle because of ignoring God's command through Necho, king of Egypt (2 Chronicles 35:21-24).

In like manner, many people will ultimately inherit wrath for rejecting the Lord Jesus as their Savior (Matthew 13:46-48; 25:46; John 3:18; 5:27-29; Hebrews 10:26-31; 12:25; Revelation 20:12-15). The Bible also warns us against the evil that is planned against us through trials and persecutions (Jeremiah 38:6; John 16:33) and God encourages us to rejoice in such sufferings (Romans 5:3-5; 1 Peter 1:6-9; James 1:2-4).

The Lord chastises those He loves, and this leads us to repentance (Hebrews 12:6; Revelation 3:19), but we should not confuse God's discipline of his children with the consequences of sin. From reading the Old Testament, we learn that sin was punished almost immediately (Joshua 7:24-25). There was an immediate judgment to preserve the fear of God in the community. However, the dispensation of grace that came through our Lord Jesus Christ is allowed to continue the way it does. The Bible says that the Lord has set a day aside to finally judge all rebellion (2 Thessalonians 1:3-11). Since there will be consequences, let us embrace this marvelous act of God's grace and not take advantage of it (2 Corinthians 6:1; 2 Peter 2:4-9). Sin still results in evil consequences (Galatians 6:8), the ultimate and severest of which is death (Romans 6:23).

God Our Comforter

In this evil world, bad things happen to the righteous and the ungodly alike (Ecclesiastes 9:2-3). However, for the righteous, God stands ready to provide us with the help we need, if we wholly trust Him (Psalm 50:15; 91:15; 121:1-2). The Lord promised that He would never leave those who trust in Him, nor forsake those whose faith is in Him (Hebrews 13:5).

Experiencing trouble is very discomforting. Given the unpredictable nature of life, sometimes we are directly responsible for the trouble and on other times we are just innocent victims. Regardless of the nature and extent of the trouble we face, we have God to comfort us and to deliver us, as He did for Job, Naomi, Daniel, and many others. As we know it, trouble is unavoidable in this life and an evil day is reserved for mankind (Ecclesiastes 9:12). But as children of God, we know God uses the evil that was intended against us and turns it into comfort for us and His glory (Genesis 50:20). God does not bring evil; He works against evil for our good (Isaiah 9:6; Romans 8:28). If we are encircled by evil as Daniel was, we should not give up our faith and hope in Him, for during that hour we will experience His power and love for us (Daniel 6:21-22).

Throughout the entire Bible, God emphatically promises deliverance (Psalm 91:1-16; Isaiah 43:2; Job 5:19). Therefore, brace yourself for deliverance when you trust in God in the day of trouble (Psalm 27:5; 50:15)! It is not right to blame God when bad things happen to us. The Lord warns us that, bad things are bound to happen, through temptations or otherwise (Matthew 18:7), but the one through whom it comes, Satan or his servant they will be held responsible. While trouble is inevitable, it might become an opportunity for us to reach out to God for help and seek His grace of deliverance which should encourage us to obedient living (John 5:14; 8:10-11).

The truth is this: Following the Lord Jesus was never a guarantee that we will be trouble-free in this world. In their prophetic teachings, to Christians, Paul, Peter, James and the Lord Jesus Christ foretold that suffering would be part of our salvation package (Romans 5:3; 1 Peter 4:12-19; James 1:2; John 15:20).

Let us, therefore, stop blaming God when bad things happen to us, because this only stores up judgment against us. Is your situation blinding you to make God your scapegoat when He promises to help us? Do you think God genuinely intends to cause us pain, trouble, and conflict, when He commands us to come to Him for comfort (Matthew 11:28-29)? Brethren, we must acknowledge the existence of evil and that bad things are as a result of evil. God plays no malicious role; His intention is to genuinely rescue us from all evil and things that trouble us. This is why He will create a new beginning – a heaven and a new earth – and wipe away all our tears (Revelation 21:1-4).

As a parent, I would not like to cause pain to any of my children. Do you genuinely believe that God delights in our troubles? The Lord Himself says: *"I have no pleasure in the death of the wicked, but that the wicked turn from his way and live"*, and He urgently pleads with us to *"Turn, turn from your evil ways! For why should you die...?"* (Ezekiel 18:32; 33:11 NKJV)? The Lord Jesus encourages us to be "faithful servants" who are always ready and prepared (Matthew 24:45-51; 25:19-23). He has already forewarned us that things will only get progressively worse as His return nears (Matthew 24:1-35; 2 Timothy 3:5; Revelation 8:13).

CHAPTER 12

Blaming God When Bad Things Happen – Part II

Do not be deceived, God is not mocked; for whatever a man sows, that he will also reap (Galatians 6:7 NKJV).

As we mentioned in the previous chapter, we cannot exhaustively answer the timeless question of why bad things happen to good people, but the Bible tells us that Satan is the prime source of all human problems. In this chapter, we will continue to share our convictions and experiences with the Lord Jesus Christ, as well as the understanding that God has imparted to us through the Holy Spirit and studying the Scriptures. We will share from Scripture how people consciously choose to go against God's counsel and reap the consequences for their choices. We will also show that since Creation and the curse (Genesis 3:17), God has allowed His creation to continue in its course of direction, and it only changes course when He intervenes for the good of humanity (Joshua 10:13; Exodus 14:21).

Life, as we know it, does not promise a smooth path (John 16:33). The Scriptures tell us that this came about after man was ejected from Eden—the Garden of God Almighty and the place of exceeding abundance. The world of suffering was the price for disobedience. The Garden of Eden is now nowhere to be found on this earth. Since there were spiritual beings guarding it, the Garden of God is in the spiritual realm of the Heavens (Genesis 3:23-24). This is where the tree of life is—in the New Jerusalem—God's new creation, where there will be no more sin and no more curse (Revelation 21:27; 22:3).

Ignorance of the order of events as God ordained them has caused much confusion and, consequently, wrecked the faith of countless Christians. Since God allowed His Son to suffer so much for us to be re-united with Him, then this is serious love—He truly intends to save us from the curse! The order of life on this earth has been ordained to run its course until the dispensation of the new order or creation (Revelation 21:5). So, there is hope – a renewal is coming, the true reign of peace that all creation longs for! (Isaiah 11:1-9; Romans 8:18-23; Revelation 21:1-5).

God's Care for Man

Out of His love for humanity, God has always acted in the best interest of people (Genesis 9:3; 1 Timothy 6:17). The evidence of His great love for humanity has been well demonstrated in the Creation account, in that after He created everything He gave it all to humanity to eat, enjoy and rule over all the work of His hands (Genesis 1:26). Even after our first parents disobeyed God (Genesis 3:6-8) and subsequently faced His judgments, He still showed care for their well-being (Genesis 3:21). Because of man's sin, *"...the whole creation groans and labors with birth pangs..."* (Romans 8:22 NKJV). So when people ask, "why is there increase in natural disasters these days?" we know this "groaning" is because the Lord's coming is near. The Bible forewarns that there will be increased distress, signs from heaven, and fearful events including dreadful weather and natural disasters (Daniel 12:1; Mark 13:8; Luke 21:11). Nature has been in rebellion against humanity in various seasons and operating against the human will and wishes. That perfect balance between man and nature was changed when God cursed the ground (Genesis 3:18; 8:22).

As it is, this move brought about limitations and sufferings (Genesis 3:18). Although God had lived and walked with men (Genesis 3:8-10), humanity's problems were further increased when God withdrew from sinful man as wickedness increased (Genesis 6:3-7). The Bible tells us that there is fullness of joy in the Presence of the Lord (Psalm 16:11). After the curse and God's withdrawal from humanity, this fullness and joy were replaced with pain, suffering, and a rebellious nature. In other words, the curse is in perpetual obedience to the command of God who alone has power to reverse it (Genesis 3:14-19; Romans 8:20). In His infinite wisdom, God elects to intervene upon request, to avert a potentially destructive situation or turn it in our favor (Jonah 1:11-15; Matthew 8:23-27). This is what we are experiencing today. Grace is given by God's choice (Romans 9:15), and He intervenes in our trials and testing situations (Acts 12:11). He grants requests to save and deliver all who ask and believe in Him (John 6:37; Psalm 91:15).

God is not working against us, but He teaches us to appreciate Him and to show us that those who put their trust in Him have security and true peace (Isaiah 46:4; 43:2; Deuteronomy 31:6; Romans 8:31; Ephesians 2:14). There are many enemies of truth, including some Christians, who blame God for all bad things. If we have faith in a Just and Loving God, then it is unthinkable to accuse Him of perpetuating trouble when He promises to help us when we call on Him (Psalm 50:15; Job 34:10).

God's counsel to humanity after the dispensation of the curse required man to fight and overcome sinful and rebellious nature (Genesis 4:7). Humanity was left weak when God withdrew His Spirit, leaving man to fight against sin, which sets man's conscience alight with guilt, and where guilt is there is an absence of peace. As we know, it is in God alone that we enjoy enduring peace (Exodus 33:14; Isaiah 26:3), so an absence of God results in hardships and emotional distress (1 Samuel 16:14). The good news is that even though we may face suffering even until death (Revelation 2:10), God has already fulfilled His promise to give us victory over Satan (Genesis 3:15) by sending His Only Begotten Son, Jesus Christ, to save us and "crush" Satan (John 3:16; Romans 16:20). The reality of our choice should be to obey the Lord because we know that despite all the challenges we face, only He has Sovereign power over everything, thus showing creation's dependence on Him for existence (Romans 8:20-22).

What Does God Expect from Us?

One day, while I was out witnessing and handing out Gospel tracts, an elderly man I witnessed to asked me what God wants from us. In reply, my answer to him was that God was calling upon all men everywhere to repent, meaning forsaking sin and preparing for His Kingdom in anticipation of the final judgment (Acts 17:30-31). After hearing this, the man nodded in acknowledgment and went away.

God does not "force" us to do His will by holding people to ransom to change the course of things only when we turn to Him. Instead, He gives us choices and consequences (Deuteronomy 30:15, 19; Joshua 24:15). For example, the people of Nineveh chose to repent from their sins and the Lord forgave them and relented from the punishment planned for them. Additionally, from our personal experiences, when we have asked the Lord to come to our rescue in a given testing situation, He has often allowed us to go through that situation and somehow changed the outcome in our favor (Daniel 3:24-27; 6:21-23). A family might go through the painful experience of having their property repossessed or foreclosed by the bank, but God may use this situation as a means to get them out of financial debt and bring glory to Him (Romans 8:28). No one is exempt from facing various troubles, and even our Lord and Savior Jesus Christ experienced trials (Luke 22:28; James 1:2; 1 Peter 1:6). However, today many people, including Christians, are made to believe that they do not have to go through the pain of creation's curse and that Christ took all pains for us. Yes, He did regarding God's judgment, but not regarding what I call 'earthly tax,' which is our cup of suffering (Job 14:1). Contrary to popular teachings that Christians should have bliss and ease in this world (prosperity, wealth, and health, etc.), the Bible categorically warns us that followers of Christ will face hardships, sufferings, tribulations, trials, and disappointments in this world. We are called to endure and persevere to the very end (John 16:33; Romans 5:3-5; 8:18; 1 Peter 4:12-19; 5:10; James 1:2-4; 2 Corinthians 4:8-10; Revelation 21:4).

Even though we cannot escape facing stressful challenges, we can rejoice and experience peace when we allow God in our lives to go with us through our troubles, which makes it more bearable and so rewarding (Exodus 14:21-31; Psalm 23:4). In other words, God is saying there is a cup of trouble stirred up for each one of us in life, but we will see and experience His love and care for us when we go with Him like the bold and fearless Shadrach, Meshach, and Abednego (Daniel 3:16-18; Ecclesiastes 9:12; Psalm 55:22; Isaiah 43:2).

Disobedience Reverses God's Plan for Us

God disciplines or chastens His children in an act of love to draw us back to Him (Proverbs 3:12; Hebrews 12:6-7). There is a distinction between the punishment of God and the consequences of sin fueled by Satan's deceptions. We all suffer the consequences of the sinful choices we make, but God is willing to forgive us and help us heal. Blaming God when we rebelliously or ignorantly make bad decision after ample warnings is outright unjust, selfish, and foolish. The Lord never works against His obedient children. If He initiated the plan of salvation, giving us the weapons and tools to secure a victorious experience, how is it justifiable to charge Him with wrongdoing (Genesis 18:25-36)? We may say God allows things to happen to us, but blaming Him as the cause of our problems is blasphemous and unappreciative of His blessings. As with Daniel, David, and others, He allows painful experiences to give us the benefit of His love, joy, and ever-present care.

God does not lie or change His counsels, purposes, and decrees (Numbers 23:19), nor does He change His plans for us (Jeremiah 29:11). It is us, as a result of the choices we make in defiance or disobedience to His will, who alter our course of direction (1 Kings 11:37-38; 14:7-11). King Saul, for example, could not maintain a faithful relationship with God, and he missed God's promises and blessings (1 Samuel 15:10-26). When the Israelites failed to obey God's commands, He allowed the other nations to inflict hardship on them and to prevail against them (Psalm 78:59; Judges 3:7-11). Likewise, King Jeroboam was given a promise by God that he and his sons would have a lasting dynasty in Israel if he would obey the Lord. However, he sinned and lost the promise, which resulted in a judgment against him (1 Kings 11:26-39; 14:7-16).

Have you been blaming God for all your troubles and growing further away from Him? Have you been under attack from the enemy and feel that God is far from you? Do you want to become a child of God who will overcome evil? Our Heavenly Father has reserved just love for the entire human race. Please call on the Lord, repent, put your trust in Him, and allow the joy of His concern for you to bring deliverance and carry you through the trap of life's uncertainties (Ecclesiastes 7:14). *The LORD is gracious and compassionate, slow to anger and rich in love* (Exodus 34:6; Psalm 145:8 NIV). So, *"Let the wicked forsake his way, and the unrighteous man his thoughts; Let him return to the Lord, and He will have mercy on him; And to our God, for He will abundantly pardon"* (Isaiah 55:7 NKJV).

CHAPTER 13

Allow God's Righteous Judgment

"Friends, do not avenge yourselves; instead, leave room for His wrath.
For it is written: Vengeance belongs to me; I will repay, says the Lord"
(Romans 12:19 NKJV)

Revenge is Hatred

Naturally, the spirit of revenge is well embedded in most of us. This is evident by our desire to give or receive some remedy for some pain or loss we suffered. Biblically, it is not wrong to desire justice (Deuteronomy 16:18), since God established this principle in our hearts. Our response to someone who has acted wrongfully against us is often motivated by our sense of how justice should be meted out, and often our own prejudices will deny the offending person a fair opportunity to receive a just recourse. As it is, when we seek justice for ourselves against a cause or someone, our appreciation for justice is influenced by our feelings, which may give rise to injustice against the other person. For example, as part of the due process of law, most courts carefully examine all available evidence in a bid to establish the truth before drawing a conclusion and awarding a decision for or against an accused or an accuser. While our human courts are limited in establishing the truthfulness in most matters of dispute, their decisions still play a crucial role in society by enforcing positive actions while discouraging self-motivating, negative reactions. Therefore, the role the governing authorities play in discouraging arbitrary actions in society helps in maintaining some order and solving disputes (Romans 13:1-5).

The Lord has commanded us not to pursue revenge against anyone who has wronged us (Leviticus 19:18; Romans 12:17). He instructs us to overcome evil with good (Romans 12:21). Our response should not be to inflict harm, which would render us guilty before God. Understandably, when we are wronged, we argue in our defense and often our motive is to mete out what we think or believe is due revenge. The Lord commands us not to seek revenge; He knows that hateful feelings often motivate us, and this is evil. At best, revenge is an expression of intended hateful feelings to cause harm. If we act from revenge, we leave no room for corrective action, mercy, and forgiveness; these are some of the remedies God gave to society (Matthew 18:32-35).

As a fact, we are often told that Christians must not take one another to court because the Bible says *"If any of you has a dispute with another, do you dare to take it before the ungodly for judgment instead of before the Lord's people?"* (1 Corinthians 6:1 NIV). We need to understand that the apostle Paul was referring to disputes in the church and among brethren and not matters relating to social issues in society (1 Corinthians 6:5-6). In fact, when the Jewish religious authorities persecuted Paul, he wisely used the governing authorities of the day to help him find justice and to defend his faith (Acts 22-26). Furthermore, kindly allow me to clarify. It is always good to forgive an offender unconditionally; however, the Lord does not command us not to pursue justice through our courts. This would be of course after first seeking peaceful solutions from our offenders and authorities in our communities. When we pursue a matter legally, especially where we voluntarily and contractually went into an agreement, our motive should be to seek action or compliance to settle our dispute with the other person and not as a cause of revenge. Legally, we allow an independent person with knowledge about certain laws governing our relations to play an arbitration role and decide a matter between an offender and a plaintiff, in the interest of peaceful cohabitation. Various teachings in the Bible encourage social justice (Exodus 18:24-26; 1 Kings 3:16-28; 2 Samuel 15:2; Isaiah 1:17).

How Worldly Movies Encourage Revenge

Many films and TV shows use revenge as the main plot, and this is often very violent and brutal, and subtly provokes an evil spirit of anger in their audience. This has also contributed to desensitizing Christians on the seriousness of this sin. As God-fearing Christians, the Lord expects us to judge our motives in the light of His Word, giving love and forgiveness to an offender and pointing them to correction (2 Timothy 3:16). As it is, the Lord Himself taught and clarified that we should extend love and forgiveness even to our enemies (Matthew 5:38-48). While the death of saints (the righteous) is precious in the sight of the Lord as they are reunited with Him in everlasting peace (Psalm 116:15), He also takes no pleasure (or delight) in the death of the wicked. God's desire for the wicked is for them to repent and turn away from their wicked ways so that they may live (Ezekiel 18:23; 33:11). God loves all His children so much (John 3:16), that He *"causes His sun to rise on the evil and the good, and sends rain on the righteous and the unrighteous"* (Matthew 5:45 NIV).

Allow God to Revenge and Fight Your Cause

A few years ago, some evil men viciously assaulted and abused a very faithful member of our ministry, leaving this precious sister physically paralyzed and with emotional scars. From what we have witnessed, the abuse she suffered would provoke any person to harbor hateful feelings and unforgiveness. However, this precious sister opted to obey the Lord and forgive her offenders without reservations. She shared with us that the night she was attacked and hospitalized, the Lord appeared in a vision to her at her bedside and commanded her to forgive the men who had abused and assaulted her and that He would punish them for what they did to her. As you may imagine, she was still coming to terms with her ordeal with the wounds and pain still fresh in her mind, yet God asked her to forgive; she confessed that she was somewhat confused but not bitter, and she forgave them.

It is a fact that some people find it very hard to forgive offenders immediately because some of us still need to work through it emotionally. In my work as a minister of the gospel, I have personally counseled many people who found it very difficult to forgive others and some needed weeks, months and even years to work through their hateful feelings. Often, unforgiveness leads some people to curse and wish bad things on those who offended them. Some even revenge by withholding forgiveness. Their minds are focused on repaying evil and to their loss. Beloved, as we shared in our *Being Humble* message (please refer to our website), if the Lord comes, or we died, while still struggling to forgive, we might be denied entry into Heaven! The Lord Jesus clearly warns us that if we do not forgive others their sins, our Father will not forgive our sins either (Matthew 6:15; Luke 11:26). Therefore, it is in our best interest to *"bear with each other and forgive one another if any of you has a grievance against someone. Forgive as the Lord forgave you"* (Colossians 3:13 NIV).

Three years into our ministry, the Lord sent three of our daughters, who were between ten and twelve years old at the time, to witness and share the gospel in a certain area. While they were busy handing out Gospel tracts, a man approached them and, without warning, took off his belt and started spanking them in public for no reason. Being humiliated, they did not utter a word against their attacker. Instead, the Lord provided an elderly woman to rebuke their assailant. When the Lord visited Charis that evening, He said that they should forgive the man who had attacked them and that He would repay the offender.

I also once endured an attack. What made the situation uncomfortable is that I had to forgive and share my house with a young man who maliciously and violently attacked me. The attack left me permanently disabled and fractured in my right hand with four of my fingers badly deformed and nonfunctional. To help me forgive my attacker, I repeatedly heard the Lord in an audible voice saying, *"But anyone who hates a brother or sister is in the darkness and walks around in the darkness. They do not know where they are going, because the darkness has blinded them"* (1 John 2:11 NIV). Admittedly, I harbored strong feelings of hatred and I wanted to take revenge against the young man. However, I persisted in prayer daily asking the Lord to forgive me and to deliver me from those hateful feelings. Within a few weeks, I received my deliverance by praying against and resisting those hateful feelings every time they came over me until the Lord set me free and replaced those bitter feelings with compassion and love for the young man.

Likewise, another sister in the ministry was emotionally hurt and offended by a relative. She found herself arguing and debating daily in her mind with this relative while harboring ill feelings towards her. The way she received deliverance was by acknowledging this as a sin before God each morning, and asking for God's help not to argue in her mind with her relative during the day (Psalm 50:15). Each time she would start debating in her mind, she would choose to repent, ask for forgiveness, forgive the relative, and pray blessings over her (Luke 6:27-28; 31). She did this for a few weeks until the Lord delivered her from this bondage. She no longer debates with her relative but feels peace towards her and is praying for the relative's salvation.

Please do not allow the devil to deceive you! Some of the skillful devices the devil uses are to make us feel sorry for ourselves and have us think that others (our offenders) are taking advantage of us especially if we choose to love and forgive them. We might be looked at as fools, but we are preciously living out the values the Lord taught and stood for. We, therefore, encourage you to leave room for God's wrath (Romans 12:19) and allow Him to sanctify you in His truth and will. Let us remember not to allow revenge to steal your salvation! This is not worthwhile since our years of faithful service in the Lord are about to be rewarded soon! *And in whatever [we] do, [let us] work at it with all [our hearts], as working for the Lord, not for human masters, since [we] know that [we] will receive an inheritance from the Lord as a reward. It is the Lord Christ [we] are serving. Anyone who does wrong will be repaid for their wrongs, and there is no favoritism (Colossians 3:23-25 NIV).*

Have you been harboring grudges against anyone, and seeking payback or revenge in your own terms? Are you trapped in anger and unforgiveness against someone who wronged you? Remember, vengeance belongs to God (Deuteronomy 32:35; 43; Psalm 94:1-2 NKJV). Some great men of God like Paul and King David knew this, and although they were wronged, they left vengeance to God (2 Timothy 4:14; 1 Samuel 26:10-11). Our Savior and Lord Jesus Christ endured much hostility from sinners against Himself, yet He did not retaliate but forgave even while on the cross (1 Peter 2:23; Hebrews 12:3-4; Luke 23:34). The Bible admonishes us neither to say, *"I'll pay you back for this wrong!"* (Proverbs 20:22 NIV), nor to say, *"I'll do to them as they have done to me; I'll pay them back for what they did"* (Proverbs 24:29 NIV) but *"Wait for the Lord, and He will avenge you"* (Proverbs 20:22 NIV). I conclude this chapter by encouraging you with these words from the Lord to us: *"I am READY to come – SOON!"*

CHAPTER 14

The Sin of Adultery

Whoever divorces his wife and marries another commits adultery; and
whoever marries her who is divorced from her husband commits adultery
(Luke 16:18 NKJV)

The Lord has warned us in His Word about adultery, yet many Christians still practice this sin with reckless abandon. Adultery is defined as any voluntary sexual intercourse between someone who is married, with another person whom he/she is not married to (someone else who is not his or her spouse). Similar to the sin of adultery is fornication – the voluntary sexual intercourse between persons (single or married) who are not married to each other. This chapter addresses adultery, but the same applies to fornication and other sexual sins.

Besides the physical act of engaging in adultery, the Lord's standards are much higher, and He says that if anyone man or woman *"looks at the other person lustfully,"* he or she has already committed adultery with that person in his or her heart (Matthew 5:27-28). Today, this includes watching pornography on movies, TV, and Internet, as well as reading "adult-themed" content in magazines or online. The Word of God directly forbids these immoral practices.

The sin of adultery is committed much in the church today and, like all other sins, it is orchestrated and motivated by demons as Satan controls the world through wicked man. God has provided His Word and commandments to guide our behavior, lives, and conscience so that we may understand and recognize sinful habits and behavior (Romans 7:13). The Bible contains life-giving teachings and warnings against every sin committed by people on Earth. Let us remember that sin came into the world through an act of disobedience and rebelliousness (Romans 5:19). This rebelliousness first came through Satan (Genesis 3:1-6) and, since he is the tempter (Matthew 4:3), he spreads his dominion of disobedience by influencing people's choices, thus leading them into temptation and sin against God (Ephesians 2:2).

Since any wrongdoing must be driven by some desire, there must be a tempter present to draw us into submission and the execution of the sinful act. It is, therefore, safe to say that a sinful act is preceded by a demonic influence (2 Chronicles 18:22; Luke 22:3). The Lord in some of the visions we have shared has confirmed this understanding of how Satan influences us to sin. Brethren, these teaching are not myths; Satan operates and works through the spirit of desire. Desire is what we need to gratify our cravings at that point in time (Genesis 3:6; 2 Samuel 11:2-4). It is clear from the Bible's explanation that through some of our senses, for example through seeing, an appetite (desire) is created before engagement of the sin. Since we, as human beings, have feelings, cravings, and basic needs and wants to be satisfied, it is easy to give in to fleshly desires and sin, while rationalizing the consequences in exchange for the benefits. In other words, we would rather go against the command of our conscience in disobedience to satisfy the needs of our cravings (Hebrews 10:2). As people of faith, if we have a conscience that has not been seared, defiled, or weakened, we have the Holy Spirit who convicts us by making us feel guilty or making us feel uneasy and out of peace (2 Samuel 24:10), and the Word of God is a shield which informs our conscience against acts of disobedience (Joshua 1:8).

Adultery and its Consequences

Sexual immorality, in general, is as evil and unacceptable as murder, theft, and idolatry (Revelation 21:8). It carries the same punishment as all the other sins. The Lord warned that if a man divorces his wife, lusts after another woman, or remarries to conceal his adulterous ways, he is acting unfaithfully, and the same applies to whoever marries her who is divorced from her husband (Matthew 5:28; Luke 16:18).

We need to understand that when a man and a woman enter into marriage, the vows they take happen in God's Presence. It is He who ordained marriage between a husband and wife who acts as a Witness to this holy oneness (Matthew 19:4-9; Malachi 2:14-16). One is released from the covenant marriage if a spouse dies, and in this case, God will honor and bless the second marriage for one whose spouse has passed away and is marrying another person who is not divorced; otherwise adultery or fornication is committed (Matthew 5:32; Romans 7:2). Remarrying as a result of divorce may be legal, but the Bible says that it also committing adultery (Matthew 19:9; 1 Corinthians 7:1-11).

The Lord does not become a Witness between us if we have broken faith and had gone against the counsel of His Word and commandment (Malachi 2:14-16). His plan for marriage was for it to be a permanent union, or marriage *covenant*, between one man and one woman, and the two becoming one flesh, as it was in the beginning with Adam and Eve (Genesis 2:21-25; Matthew 19:1-9). In the Bible, covenants were not meant to be broken under any circumstance – for example when the Gibeonites deceived the Israelites into signing a covenant, both had to live with the consequences of their agreement (Joshua 9:14-20), to the extent that when Gibeonites were under attack, the Israelites had to defend them since they had signed a covenant (Joshua 10:3-10). However, when King Saul in his zeal for Israel broke the conditions of the covenant that Joshua and the elders of Israel made with the Gibeonites by an oath in God's Presence, the Lord struck the land with a crippling famine that lasted three successive years (Joshua 9:14-15;2 Samuel 21:1). From what we observed in some second marriages, there is no peace and unity, and a second marriage has higher chances of breaking than the first one. Also, second marriages introduce new family feuds and insecurity, and often the children are on the receiving end of such conflict (Malachi 2:16). As it is, peace from God is absent because of our disobedience to Him (Isaiah 48:22).

Shamefully, today's generation sees marriage as a contract (conditional and revocable), as opposed to a covenant (unconditional and irrevocable). As the Lord clearly said, Moses permitted the Israelites to divorce because of their hardened hearts (Matthew 19:8-9; Malachi 2:13-14); but the Lord Himself indicates that He hates divorce (Malachi 2:16). As believers under the New Covenant, we should not harden our hearts, but rather have hearts of flesh (Ezekiel 11:19; 36:26) and be willing to love and forgive. Unforgiveness, lustfulness, selfishness, and jealousy are bitter roots and leading causes of divorce that should be overcome. As the Scriptures teach, if we do not forgive others of their sins, the Lord also not forgive us our sins (Luke 6:37, Matthew 6:12).

Obedience to the Lord in Marriage

For a strong foundation in marriage, the Bible encourages believers not to be unequally yoked with unbelievers (2 Corinthians 6:14). Once married, the Christian couple should submit to the Lord, love each other as oneself and as Christ loves the Church, and also have respect for each other (Ephesians 5:22-33). If we do this, there will be fewer problems.

My wife and I counseled a close relative back in 2011 regarding marriage. He had a desire to serve the Lord, but he was not legally divorced from his previous wife and was living in sin with another woman. Since the Bible forbids divorce and remarriage, we were lost on how to help him find a solution. Therefore, we turned to the Lord, and He said, *"My son Adrian must do the right thing."* By this, the Lord meant that he should obey the Scriptures, by either reconciling with his estranged wife or remaining single (1 Corinthians 7:11). Similarly, after learning how good the Lord was to us, a single mother who lived with a married man asked if she might join our prayer group. We honestly did not want to hurt her after seeing her enthusiasm, but we had to obey the Lord, so we counseled her first to make right with the Lord and repent of the sin of adultery. Our Christian duty was to correct her Scripturally to do the right thing, and then come and serve the Lord in peace and with a clear conscience. Because sin is so deceitful and addictive, she never followed our counsel. This is breaking the heart of the Lord. There are many people who desire to serve the Lord, but at the same time, they do not want to let go of their sins. We cannot serve God and the cravings of sin at the same time (Matthew 6:24). Some worldly people might construe our correction to the woman as judging. However, we were not judging her but applied the Scriptures to correct her. It is our Christian duty to use the Sword of the Spirit as a measuring rod to dispel error. Also, the Scriptures teach on correcting others (1 Timothy 5:20; 2 Timothy 4:2; Galatians 6:1; Hebrews 10:24; 2 Thessalonians 3:15). The Lord confirmed this through a vision warning believers not to use His Name in vain and encouraging us to rebuke one another when we do wrong things so that we can be saved from hell. It is not us, or one issuing a correction, who judges; it is His Word.

In another case regarding divorce, one faithful sister in our ministry requested us to inquire of the Lord if she could divorce her husband because of his infidelities and abusive attitude. The Lord discouraged her not to seek a divorce, and instead He told her to continue praying for her husband. She obeyed, and the Lord brought them back together!

Forgiveness and Salvation for Remarried People

You might ask, "What if I am divorced and I remarried. Does that mean I am excluded from becoming a born-again Christian?" This is a good question that might be puzzling many other people out there. I surely do not like to be viewed as misrepresenting the word of God here, nor do I want to be seen *"shutting the Kingdom in people's faces"* (Matthew 23:13 NIV). In the whole Bible, no direct provision has been made for incidents like this, except for adultery (Matthew 5:32). However, this does not explicitly endorse remarriage (Luke 16:18). I have been wondering for a long time on the fate of Christians who married, divorced, and remarried. During my personal Bible study sessions, I was drawn to the following Bible verses:

"Let each one remain in the same calling in which he was called. Were you called while a slave? Do not be concerned about it; but if you can be made

free, rather use it. For he who is called in the Lord while a slave is the Lord's freedman. Likewise, he who is called while free is Christ's slave. You were bought at a price; do not become slaves of men. Brethren, let each one remain with God in that state in which he was called" (1 Corinthians 7:20-24 NKJV).

I wondered if these verses applied to people who remarried before they became born again. As much as I knew, they must have been living in disobedience by divorcing and remarrying. I was disturbed and wondered if there must be some forgiveness for them if the Lord did not close the door of salvation on them. I did not want to wrongly apply the above Bible verses to their situation since they do not explicitly say so. In our petition to the Lord Jesus Christ regarding this matter, He gave the following directives in the two short visions below.

Vision Given to Charis on July 31, 2013: Remaining as First Called

"On July 31, 2013, we prayed in agreement as a family and my father asked me to ask the Lord if 1 Corinthians 7:17-24 applies to people who were once married, divorced and remarried. That evening during the Lord's regular visits, I (Charis) saw the Lord coming down from Heaven on a cloud, and He had a pure white robe on with a sash across His chest reading KING OF KINGS and LORD OF LORDS. He was standing at the usual place where we usually met during His visits to me. However, this night I was standing in front of the Lord with my Bible opened on 1 Corinthians 7:17-24. While the Lord was standing there, I asked the Lord the question that my father had phrased for me (see above) while I pointed with my finger to the above verses in the Bible, just as we agreed in prayer. Without hesitation, the Lord answered and said, *"YES! This Scripture applies to people in that situation."* I said, "Thank you, Lord!" The Lord replied, *"It's a Pleasure My daughter"* and He proceeded to tell me to inform my father to put it on the website for all to read and know. After this, I closed my Bible, put it under my arms, and just as I left I saw how the Lord ascended to Heaven." End of vision.

We were concerned about the possible abuse of this provision, so we also asked the Lord again to issue a warning since there might be people who use God's grace to indulge in sin. In emphasis, this provision strictly applies to people who were divorced and remarried before they became Christians. In other words, their divorce and remarriage happened before they knew the Lord. The Lord grants them this provision to allow them salvation. Here is the warning from the Lord:

Vision Given to Charis on August 5, 2013: Warning on Disobedience

"I was given a follow-up vision on adultery as a warning by the Lord to Christians in the early hours of August 5, 2013. I was in a pure white room, and in the room, there was a memory stick and a DVD player which was suspended in midair. I took the flash drive and inserted it into the DVD player. At once, I heard a recorded message saying, *"People who know My teachings and disobey Me and do wrong things will be severely punished!"*. For confirmation, I asked, "Is it the Lord Jesus speaking?" The voice said through the recording, *"Yes, it is the Lord Jesus Christ speaking, go now and don't forget!"* I replied and said, "Yes Lord, I will tell my father." The vision ended.

Beloved, if the Lord calls us, we should not continue in sin (1 John 3:9; Revelation 21:8). Through the above vision and warning, every Christian who disobeys and uses this Scripture (1 Corinthians 7:18-24) to remarry will be subject to judgment and punishment. Do not play with your salvation; obey the Lord!

CHAPTER 15

Prayer of Repentance

We would like to conclude this book by inviting you to make Jesus your Lord and Savior. He loves you very much and the messages He has given us are for you.

If you want to turn from your present way of life, please pray the prayer below from your heart by faith. God will listen and save you from Hell. After you have prayed in repentance, kindly follow the instructions below to grow in truth, obedience and bear spiritual fruit for service. This short prayer can change your life forever!

Heavenly Father, I bow my head in submission to your will and admit that I am a sinner, destined for HELL if I die without having accepted Jesus Christ as my eternal Lord and Savior. I acknowledge that I cannot save myself and I need a redeemer. I completely repent of my sins and put my faith in the blood of the Lord Jesus Christ shed for my sins on the cross. I NOW accept Jesus Christ as my Savior. Lord Jesus, please fill me with your Holy Spirit. I trust that You will appear soon to take me to Heaven for all eternity. In Jesus' name, AMEN.

After you have prayed this prayer, we encourage you to be a faithful believer by doing the "Duties of a True Born Again Christian." Please visit our website or read Book 1 for more information on the duties of true Christian, especially reading your Bible daily (Joshua 1:8; 1 Peter 2:2), praying at least three times per day (Daniel 6:10; Psalm 55:17), and Witnessing (Mark 16:15). Please be obedient and live the Word!

About the Author

Glenn K van Rooyen first committed his life to the Lord Jesus Christ in February 1990. In 1992, he received a personal visitation from the Lord Jesus Christ. After the Lord had shown him the marks of the cross on His right hand, he asked the Lord some questions, and in response, the Lord Jesus referred him to the Bible as the only source of Truth.

After backsliding for more than ten years, Brother Glenn recommitted his life to the Lord in January 2008 following severe hardships. After he started faithfully seeking the Lord again, he and his wife, along with their first-born daughter, started a home fellowship for the family in 2009. After being invited by their local church to participate in a seven-day fast in January 2010, the Lord Jesus Christ gloriously appeared to his then nine-year-old daughter Charis and said, "*I am your Lord Jesus Christ, and I will appear to you in visions and give you messages, and you must tell your father, and I love My children.*"

This was the beginning of the Lord's visits to this family, which spanned over a period of more than four years. The Lord visited almost every night, giving them teachings and visions, which we now share.

Van Rooyen Family (Left to Right): Desiree, Cailin, Glenn, Claudia, Charis, and Jaydeen

www.ingramcontent.com/pod-product-compliance
Lightning Source LLC
Chambersburg PA
CBHW071818020426
42331CB00007B/1525